TRUMP

and the

JEWS

DAVID RUBIN

Trump and the Jews
ISBN 978-0-9829067-7-4

Published by Shiloh Israel Press

Copyright © 2018 by David Rubin

www.ShilohIsraelChildren.org
www.DavidRubinIsrael.com
www.Facebook.com/DavidRubin.Shiloh.Israel

Contact The Author
David@ShilohIsraelChildren.org
1-845-738-1522

Contact The Publisher
sipress@ShilohIsraelChildren.org

For Orders
1-800-431-1579 (toll-free)

Book Development and Production
Chaim Mazo – chaim.mazo@gmail.com

Cover Design and Layout
Christopher Tobias

Printed in The United States Of America

You know, to just be grossly generalistic, you could put half of Trump's supporters into what I call the basket of deplorables. Right? The racist, sexist, homophobic, xenophobic, Islamophobic – you name it. And unfortunately, there are people like that.

(Hillary Clinton)

Trump and the Jews is dedicated to the so-called "Basket of Deplorables". Growing up in supposedly sophisticated New York City, I viewed from a distance "the hicks" and "the rednecks" who lived in other parts of the country. According to the common wisdom, they were ignorant, country bumpkin racists and even anti-Semites.

Some forty years later, having lived in Israel for twenty-six years, during which time I have visited almost every American state on my speaking tours, I am convinced that such an understanding of middle America was seriously biased, not due to malice, but definitely based on an intolerant worldview that many on the Left possess.

Hillary Clinton's statement, made during the 2016 presidential campaign, succinctly expressed that unfortunate bias, which is as bigoted as the worldview that it claims to find so detestable.

I hereby dedicate this book to the "Basket of Deplorables", the millions of Americans who still believe in God, liberty, the traditional family, and the bond between America and Israel.

Contents

"David Rubin's *Trump and the Jews* is a powerful and true account of President Trump's transformation of America's relationship with Israel, creating a new opportunity for peace. A great read!"

Christopher Ruddy – CEO of Newsmax Media

"David Rubin is a voice that needs to be heard. His *Trump and the Jews* is a timely, perhaps urgent, assessment of where we stand politically between America and Israel in the age of Trump. This in an important book, even a wake-up call whichever way one leans politically. Agree or disagree, it's a riveting read!"

Jack Engelhard – Best-Selling Novelist,
Author of "Indecent Proposal"

"Ever since the horrific attacks on 9-11, our nation has been faced with threats from abroad and from within. These dangers have only gotten worse with the passage of time. With his strong approach to border control, and his courageous determination to stand with America's allies in the Middle East, President Trump is protecting our nation's security interests. Author David Rubin is a terror victim himself, wounded together with his then three-year-old son, who was shot in the head. From the front lines of the struggle against terrorism, David Rubin has written a fascinating book, a powerful defense of the Trump presidency that should be read by every American, and by our allies in the Middle East."

Michael D. Brown – former Undersecretary, Department of
Homeland Security (DHS) and Director of FEMA

"David Rubin reveals the essence of the long-misunderstood United States-Israel relationship in all of its complexities in his new book, *Trump and the Jews*. In doing so, he obviously isn't afraid to confront the difficult issues that the Trump presidency has encountered and he does so in a way that is clear, thoughtful, and a pleasure to read!"

Eric Metaxas – #1 New York Times Best-Selling Author of "Martin Luther", "Bonhoeffer", and "If You Can Keep It"

"President Trump's support for Israel and its people goes far beyond the move of the US Embassy to Jerusalem. There have been strategic moves throughout his short presidency that have aimed at improving US-Israel relations, and making the bold statement to the world that the United States will stand behind its strongest ally. David Rubin's book *Trump and the Jews* identifies these crucial points and presents it in a way that tells the entire story seamlessly."

Dr. Robert Jeffress – Pastor, Author, Host of the syndicated television show, Pathway to Victory

"David Rubin, in his new book, *Trump and the Jews* provides a succinct education for those who desire to learn the truth and gain understanding of both the political realities and biblical mandates regarding modern Israel. This 'politically incorrect' and honest appraisal of Israel in the age of Trump provides a blueprint to solving the Israeli-Palestinian question while making the world a safer place. An invaluable contribution!"

Rick Scarborough – Founder of Vision America and Vision America Action

"I've known and admired David Rubin for a long time, beginning when he was mayor of Shiloh in Israel. Though raised in Brooklyn, he and his family have personally experienced violent terrorism in the region of Samaria, or the West Bank. No one knows Israel and its current situation better than David Rubin. He knows the American Jewish community very well – and also the fervent Evangelical support of American Christians. That includes President Trump. No one can better assess the role the Trump administration can and probably will play in Israel now than David Rubin. Read carefully!"

Pat Boone – Conservative Political Commentator
and Entertainer

The Author

Davvid Rubin is a former mayor of Shiloh, Israel – in the region of Samaria, which together with Judea, is known to much of the world as the West Bank. He is founder and president of Shiloh Israel Children's Fund (SICF) – dedicated to healing the trauma of child victims of terrorist attacks, as well as rebuilding the biblical heartland of Israel through the children. SICF was established after Rubin and his three-year-old son were wounded in a vicious terrorist attack while driving home from Jerusalem. Rubin  vowed to retaliate – not with hatred, nor with anger, but with compassion – to create positive change for Israel and its children.

Rubin's acclaimed first book, *God, Israel, & Shiloh,* tells the story of the very human struggles and triumphs of Israel's complex but fascinating history, from slavery in Egypt to the present. Rubin describes Israel's miraculous return to its biblical heartland, and the amazing challenge of rebuilding, despite the trauma of terrorism. Rubin's second book, the prophetic bestseller, *The Islamic Tsunami,* boldly exposes the danger to Israel, America and Judeo-Christian civilization posed by Jihadist Islam and its odd collusion with the secular Far Left. His third book, *Peace For Peace*, scans the history of the peace process, explaining why it has always failed, but how it can actually work – finally taking into account biblical principles, historical precedent, and common sense. Rubin's next two books, *Sparks From Zion*, and *More Sparks From Zion*, shatter the falsehoods in the mainstream media's portrayals of Israel and the Middle East. All of these books are as relevant today as when they were first published.

David Rubin appears as a frequent commentator on Fox News and Newsmax TV, as well as on many other television and radio networks, while his articles have appeared in the Jerusalem Post, Israel National News, and numerous other publications.

A featured speaker throughout North America and elsewhere, Rubin has been called the "Trusted Voice of Israel". Born and raised in Brooklyn, Rubin resides in Israel with his wife and children on a hilltop overlooking the site of Ancient Shiloh, the hallowed ground where the Tabernacle of Israel stood for three hundred and sixty-nine years, in the time of Joshua, Hannah, and Samuel the Prophet.

Introduction

We have an interesting popular expression in Israel: "Is it good for the Jews?" Whenever something momentous happens in the world, that question can be heard in the streets of Israel. In fact, when Benjamin (Bibi) Netanyahu was elected prime minister years ago, one of his campaign slogans was, "Bibi – Good for the Jews".

Many American Jews would find that expression appalling – after all, isn't it excessively parochial to talk that way? Or perhaps paranoid? Those are very reasonable questions. Do the Jewish people, who have given so much to the betterment of civilization, actually care only about themselves?

The answer to all of those questions is a resolute "No". After two thousand years of exile from the Land of Israel, the Jews have come home as a nation, returning to sovereignty in the Jewish homeland once again, but the trauma of our precarious existence in other people's lands has caused us, by necessity, to view every event through the prism of our difficult history. It's an essential survival skill that we have developed over the years. Exiled by the Romans from our country, subsequent mass beheadings of Jews on the Arabian Peninsula by Muslims, exiles and forced conversions in Spain and Portugal, followed by pogroms in Russia and the Holocaust in Europe – the threats to Jewish existence have always seemed ever-present. It certainly hasn't been easy. Nonetheless, the Jewish people have survived all of this and have even returned, in fulfillment of biblical prophecy, to reestablish Israel as a nation in its ancestral land.

Many Jewish Americans identify as Jews by religion only and squirm at any mention of a Jewish nation, but most

Israelis and many Jews in the United States would disagree, not seeing any contradiction between those two identities.

While not a Jew by any definition, Donald J. Trump is a New Yorker in the truest sense of the word. The accent, the style, the brashness, and the chutzpah – all stereotypes of the outer-borough New Yorkers – for good and for bad. The outer boroughs always radiated ethnicity, with a vast mix of immigrants from around the world. Trump's parents descended from Germany and Scotland, but many of his neighbors in the borough of Queens were Jews with family roots in Russia, Poland, Romania, and other countries.

Trump's deep connection with the Jewish people goes way back to his childhood and his father's building projects in some very Jewish neighborhoods, but it continued in his own career as a developer of massive building projects in Manhattan and other venues, and it continues to this day. What president has ever had a Jewish convert daughter, a Jewish son-in-law, and Jewish grandchildren? All that being said, why are so many American Jews in a state of panic over his presidency? Why are so many Jews actively involved in opposing his presidency with a passion that is the polar opposite of what most Israeli Jews are feeling? Last but not least, why are so many American Orthodox Jews such enthusiastic supporters? How can we explain all of these seeming contradictions?

Just in the first half of his presidency, Trump has managed to be called virtually every curse spoken on the streets of his native New York City – from racist to sexist to anti-Semite and white supremacist. Can he really be an anti-Semite given his obvious respect and affection for the State of Israel? Can he really be an anti-Semite with all of his Jewish friends, family, and close business associates? Are those charges mere politically-based slander or is there substance to them?

In *Trump and the Jews*, we will answer those questions

as we explore the complexities of Donald J. Trump. Simultaneously, we will examine and try to understand the behavior and actions of the even more complex Jewish people, both in America and in Israel.

Hopefully, by the end of *Trump and the Jews*, we will understand why so many Jews seem to instinctively hate Trump or love Trump. We will also understand why most Jews did not vote for him. These insights are invaluable for the many conservative or centrist Americans, who often are baffled by the left-wing views of so many in the Jewish community, as reflected in ideological organizations like the ACLU, or in the passionately liberal elites of Hollywood. Most importantly, American Jews will read this book and will begin to base their opinions, for or against, on the reality of the Trump presidency, not on which political club they belong to. We Jews are known to be an intelligent, educated, and rational people, so especially for us, excessive name-calling and hyperbole should be inappropriate. In short, let's explore the facts together, and then judge President Trump by the results of his presidency.

Chapter One
Founders, Presidents, And The Jews

"I had faith in Israel before it was established, I have faith in it now." [1]

(President Harry Truman, May 1948)

"Israel must recognize that it can't settle and occupy Palestinian land." [2]

(President Barack Obama, September 2016)

"When I become president, the days of treating Israel like a second-class citizen will end on day one." [3]

(Presidential Candidate Donald Trump, September 2016)

President Donald Trump's stated aspiration to strengthen the US-Israel relationship places him in good company, not only with peers like former House Speaker Newt Gingrich, Senator Ted Cruz, and former Governor Mike Huckabee, but with other great Americans who lived a long time ago. Ever since its emergence as a great nation in colonial times, the United States has had a strong connection with Israel, or at least, the heritage of the biblical nation. In fact, that biblical passion dates all the way back to the Puritans, who fled to the "New World" of America, seeking to escape what they saw as religious persecution from the church establishment in England. They were Christian immigrants who sailed to America in pursuit of religious freedom, and therefore, were called pilgrims, in recognition of their view that their destination was a "Promised Land".

The Puritans viewed their emigration from England as a virtual re-enactment of the Exodus. To them, England was Egypt, the king was the Pharaoh, the Atlantic Ocean was the Red Sea, America was the Land of Israel, and the Indians were the ancient Canaanites. The Puritans were (or considered themselves to be) the new Israelites, entering into a new covenant with God in a new Promised Land.[4]

Replacement Theology, the idea that Christians have replaced the Jews as God's chosen people resonated in the beliefs of many of these pilgrims, but, as many Christians in our times who participate in Passover Seders, they were closely influenced by Jewish ritual.

The Puritans were part of a Hebraist movement within Protestantism, learning the Bible in its original Hebrew. One of their ministers, Henry Ainsworth, studied Jewish biblical interpretation with leading rabbis during the community's (relatively) brief sojourn in Amsterdam.[5] This was shortly before their arrival in "America", during which they spent some ten years trying to find refuge in Holland. During that time, they connected with and were influenced by the Sephardic Jewish community in that country.

Thanksgiving – first celebrated in 1621, a year after the Mayflower landed – was initially conceived as a day akin to the Jewish Day of Atonement, Yom Kippur; it was to be a day of fasting, introspection and prayer, to thank the Almighty for His divine benevolence and pray for continued sustenance.[6] Before long, Thanksgiving evolved into a holiday more in the celebrative spirit of the Jewish holiday of Sukkot, which falls several days after Yom Kippur in the Jewish calendar.

"The origin of the harvest festival in England by the time the Pilgrims decided to leave was rooted in the biblical practice of the Feast of Tabernacles (Sukkot)," Dr. Paul Jehle, Executive Director of the Plymouth Rock Foundation, wrote in his book "Plymouth in the Words of Her Founders".

"Note that we do not know the original date of this event," he said, "though most suppose it to be in late October, which would correspond to the time of the Feast of Tabernacles."

"No Christian community in history identified more with the People of the Book than did the early settlers of the Massachusetts Bay Colony, who believed their own lives to be a literal reenactment of the biblical drama of the Hebrew nation," wrote noted scholar and chairman of the Jewish Bible Association Gabriel Sivan in his book "The Bible and Civilization." [7]

The earliest legislation of the colonies of New England was all determined by the Bible. For example, at the first assembly of New Haven in 1639, John Davenport clearly emphasized the primacy of the Bible as the legal and moral foundation of the colony:

"Scriptures do hold forth a perfect rule for the direction and government of all men in all duties which they are to perform to God and men as well as in the government of families and commonwealth as in matters of the Church ... the Word of God shall be the only rule to be attended unto in organizing the affairs of government in this plantation."

Subsequently, the New Haven legislators adopted a legal code – the Code of 1655 – which contained some 79 statutes, half of which included biblical references, virtually all from the Hebrew Bible. The Plymouth Colony had a similar law code as did the Massachusetts assembly, which, in 1641 adopted the so-called Capital Laws of New England based almost entirely on Mosaic law.[8]

The Hebrew Bible also played a central role in the founding of various educational institutions including Harvard, Yale, William and Mary, Rutgers, Princeton, Brown, King's College (later to be known as Columbia), Johns Hopkins, and Dartmouth. In virtually all of these colleges, the study of the Bible was required and some even adopted some Hebrew word or phrase as part of their official emblem or seal. Beneath the banner containing the Latin Lux et Veritas, the Yale seal shows an open book with the Hebrew *Urim VeTumim*, a part of the breastplate of the High Priest in the days of the Temple.

The Columbia seal has the Hebrew name for God at the top center, with the Hebrew name for one of the angels on a banner toward the middle. Dartmouth uses the Hebrew words meaning "God Almighty" in a triangle in the upper center of its seal.[9]

Dartmouth   Yale   Columbia

God and Israel in the Ivy League: There was a time when Israel and God were respected and even honored in the top American colleges. In these seals, the Hebrew language is displayed with references to God and Israel's Temple in Jerusalem. Will the thought police of the secular Left soon be demanding the removal of these words? (The Hebrew text is boxed to draw the reader's attention and is not accentuated on the official seals.)

It was permitted to give a commencement address in Hebrew at any of the above-mentioned colleges. Hebrew was a prerequisite course and having some knowledge of the language of Israel was central in the early American higher education system. Given that future presidents such as John Adams and Thomas Jefferson graduated from these institutions, it's not surprising that their connection to the God of Israel, rooted in the principles of the Old Testament, was so strong:

"We have no government armed with power capable of

contending with human passions unbridled by morality and religion. Avarice, ambition, revenge, or gallantry would break the strongest cords of our Constitution as a whale goes through a net. Our Constitution was made only for a moral and religious people. It is wholly inadequate to the government of any other."
(John Adams, speech to the US military, October 11, 1798) [10]

"God who gave us life gave us liberty. Can the liberties of a nation be secure when we have removed a conviction that these liberties are the gift of God?"
(Thomas Jefferson, Jefferson Memorial inscription) [11]

Even some 130-160 years before the establishment of the modern State of Israel, American presidents and founding fathers spoke and wrote about Israel, both biblical and modern. The founders, most of whom were Christians of deep faith, looked to biblical history for inspiration and guidance. They frequently noticed striking parallels between Israel's miraculous story and the making of the American nation. Thomas Jefferson, who would eventually become the third president, served on a committee to draft a seal for the newly-formed United States of America. This seal would characterize the spirit of the nation. He proposed the following representation:

The Children of Israel in the wilderness, led by a cloud

From Mount Sinai to Washington, DC: Moses, the Hebrew prophet and lawgiver who received the Ten Commandments, was chosen by the Architect of the Capitol to be represented on one of the 23 marble relief portraits over the gallery doors of the House Chamber in the US Capitol. Their selections depict people known for their work in establishing the principles that underlie American law.

by day, and a pillar of fire by night.[12]

Distinguished philosopher/ inventor/statesman Benjamin Franklin served on that same committee. Using the imagery of Moses lifting up his staff, and dividing the Red Sea, and Pharaoh in his chariot overwhelmed with the waters, he proposed this motto: Rebellion to tyrants is obedience to God. [13]

Franklin's analogy was actually very appropriate and matched ancient Israel's vision of leadership. Despite the fact that monarchy or dictatorship was the international norm in biblical times, Israel's form of monarchy was quite opposed to unrestricted political control.

Biblically-Based Visionary: Founding Father Benjamin Franklin derived much of his wisdom from the Torah of Israel.

After the Exodus from slavery in Egypt, the Children of Israel (the Israelites) wandered in the desert for forty years, eventually entering the Land of Israel, which was then called the Land of Canaan. Israel's leadership and unity had been torn asunder by excessive individualism following a tumultuous biblical period called the Judges. The people, in an unofficial spirit of rebellion and democracy, began to agitate for a king – a strong leader who would put an end to the painful division and instability that plagued Israel. However, this was to be no ordinary monarchy, but a monarchy with clear biblical guidelines that would obstruct Israel's eventual progression into dictatorship.

In those days, there was no king in Israel; every man did what was right in his own eyes.

(Judges 21:25)

Following Divine guidance, Samuel the Prophet cautioned the people against putting unlimited power in the hands of any one leader. He warned of the abuse of power and ruthless dictatorship that could result due to such lusting for strong leadership. But the people were not dissuaded – they persisted in their demand for a king.

They said, "No! There shall be a king over us, and we will be like all the other nations; our king will judge us, and go forth before us, and fight our wars!"

(1 Samuel 8:19-20)

The demand of the people was actually a plea for an end to the divisive Judges period. They hoped that a strong leader would bring unity and decisiveness through his leadership. The people's demand for a strong king was granted, but Samuel issued conditions that would bind the leader to a moral system of leadership, under which he would be unable to act solely according to his own whims and desires.

"If you will fear the Lord and worship Him, and hearken to His voice and not rebel against the word of the Lord, then you and the king who reigns over you will be following the Lord your God. But if you do not hearken to the voice of the Lord, and you rebel against the word of the Lord, then the hand of the Lord will be against you, and against your fathers."

(1 Samuel 12:13-15)

The biblical commentator known as the Radak teaches that the words "your fathers" in the above quote refers to the kings of Israel. In other words, Samuel was giving a clear warning that the king was expected to adhere to God's Torah. He would be held up to the same moral principles as the average citizen. For this reason, immediately upon taking office, the king was required to write his own Torah scroll and to keep it with him at all times. Thus, Samuel was showing the people who was really on the throne. Samuel made it apparent that the king was obligated to obey the guidelines given to him by the Almighty. Samuel the Prophet, two thousand years before the Magna Carta, forged what was a cutting-edge, limited monarchy, complete with a king who was given power at the democratic demand of the people. However, this king and his citizens were subservient to the Real King. This system of checks and balances was immediately tested and proven efficient, when Saul – the first King of Israel – was rapidly deposed by Samuel the Prophet for not explicitly following the instructions given to him by God during the war against Amalek, the arch-enemy of Israel.

While not a prophet, nor a president, Benjamin Franklin was a voice of morality and conscience in the American colonies. He spoke strongly against the unlimited rule of tyrants, but he also emphasized the need for leaders and citizens to follow the guidelines of Scripture as the way to constrain uncontrolled power. In lieu of prophecy as a means of enforcing human integrity, this philosophy was eventually developed into the comprehensive system of governmental self-enforcement, which included the brilliant concepts of Separation of Powers and Checks and Balances, which helped prevent abuse and corruption. However, it is important to remember that the focus on balance between strong leadership and spiritual guidance came from biblical lessons, as did the need for an enlightened, aware, and assertive citizenry.[14]

A Bible and a newspaper in every house, a good school in every district – all studied and appreciated as they merit – are the principal support of virtue, morality, and civil liberty.[15]

(Benjamin Franklin, in a letter to
the Ministry of France, March 1778)

"I will insist that the Hebrews have done more to civilize man than any other nation." [16]

(In a letter from President John Adams to Thomas Jefferson)

The letter from Adams to Jefferson is instructive in its deep gratitude that the founders had for the moral foundations

that Israel had bequeathed to the world. The very first President of the United States, George Washington, had a closeness with the Jewish community that isn't generally known to most Americans. When examining the Jewish involvement in supporting the American Revolution, one must acknowledge President Washington's close relationship with Hayim Solomon, the Polish-born Jewish American financier and revolutionary activist based in Philadelphia.

The Quiet Jew Who Financed the American Revolution: George Washington's friend Hayim Solomon loaned the modern-day equivalent of $40 billion to the newly formed American Government.

According to the research of Jacob Rader Marcus, Solomon loaned the newly-formed American government over $800,000, a sum that was never repaid. In today's market, that would be equivalent to approximately $40 billion. [17]

George Washington's appreciation for Solomon's substantial behind-the-scenes role in the Revolution may have been an important factor in GW's support for the Jewish communities of the young nation. Indeed, Solomon epitomized one of the ideal personality traits praised in the "Ethics of the Fathers" book of Jewish wisdom – "Say little, do a lot."

Washington greatly appreciated Solomon's support

for the budding nation, but his statements reveal a philosophical-historical bond with the people of Israel that seem to go much deeper. Upon Washington's election as first president of the United States, Levi Sheftall, president of the Jewish congregation in Savannah, Georgia, Kahal Kodesh Mickva Israel (Holy Congregation Hope of Israel), wrote to President Washington, on behalf of the Hebrew Congregation, "a congratulatory letter on your appointment, by unanimous approbation, to the Presidential dignity of the country." President Washington dispatched an immediate answer to the Hebrew Congregation of the City of Savannah, Georgia:

Thanked God and Thanked the Jews: Father of the nation, George Washington, believed the Scripture about blessing Israel.

"May the same wonder-working Deity, who long since delivering the Hebrews from their Egyptian Oppressors, planted them in the promised land, whose providential agency has lately been conspicuous in establishing these United States as an independent nation, still continue to water them with the dews of Heaven, and make the inhabitants of every denomination participate in the temporal and spiritual blessings of that people, whose God is Jehovah." [18]

In other words, George Washington seemed to understand that there was a clear connection between the rise of the United States as a world power and its relationship with the Jewish people. He viewed that connection as spiritually vital for the flourishing of the United States as a morally sound, economically vibrant, and powerful nation.

George Washington responds to the Savannah, Georgia Hebrew Congregation, June 14, 1790.

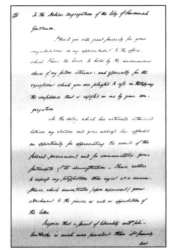

Gentlemen,

I thank you with great sincerity for your congratulations on my appointment to the office, which I have the honor to hold by the unanimous choice of my fellow-citizens: and especially for the expressions which you are pleased to use in testifying the confidence that is reposed in me by your congregation. ...

Happily the people of the United States of America have, in many instances, exhibited examples worthy of imitation ... The salutary influence of which will doubtless extend much farther, if gratefully enjoying those blessings of peace which (under favor of Heaven) have been obtained by fortitude in war, they shall conduct themselves with reverence to the Deity, and charity towards their fellow-creatures.

May the same wonder-working Deity, who long since delivering the Hebrews from their Egyptian Oppressors planted them in the promised land, whose providential agency has lately been conspicuous in establishing these United States as an independent nation, still continue to water them with the dews of Heaven and to make the inhabitants of every denomination participate in the temporal and spiritual blessings of that people whose God is Jehovah.

G. Washington

That understanding is one that is rooted in the Divine promise to Abraham, the father of the Jewish People, a biblical proclamation that Washington no doubt had learned and integrated into his worldview:

"I will bless those that bless you, and him that curses you I will curse, and all of the families of the earth shall be blessed through you..."

(Genesis 12:3)

The Philistines, the Canaanites, the Babylonians, the Romans, and many other enemies of the Jewish nation have risen and fallen, but this tiny, persecuted people has outlasted these nations that were much greater in numbers and weaponry. The Russian Empire and the great Soviet Union that treated its Jews terribly rose and fell, never reaching the levels of military prowess and economic prosperity of its American rival, the nation that provided a welcoming gateway to a land of opportunity for its Jewish immigrants, an atmosphere in which this creative, enterprising people thrived. Washington believed that the blessings that God bestowed on the United States were a result of the blessings that the United States bestowed on its Jews.

Many of Washington's successors shared that belief and deeply-felt sentiment, starting with his successor as POTUS, who expressed the Zionist vision of the rebirth of Israel as a sovereign nation in its ancestral land:

"I could find it in my heart to wish that you had been at the head of a hundred thousand Israelites ... and marching with them into Judea and making a conquest of that country and restoring your nation to the dominion of it. For I really wish the Jews (were) again in Judea an independent nation ..." [19]

(President John Adams, in a letter to Major Mordecai Manuel Noah, 1819)

(I believe in the) rebuilding of Judea as an independent nation. [20]
(John Quincy Adams)

Judea is the southern part of what most of the world now calls the West Bank – in the heart of the ancient Land of Israel. Before the Temple was destroyed by the Romans and the Jews were expelled from the Land in the year 70, Judea was the final remnant of what had once been David's unified kingdom.

Supported Israel's Return: President Abraham Lincoln expressed support for what would become, some eighty years later, the rebirth of Israel as a sovereign nation.

Not long after the Emancipation Proclamation, President Abraham Lincoln met a Canadian Christian Zionist, Henry Wentworth Monk, who expressed hope that Jews who were suffering oppression in Russia and Turkey be emancipated by restoring them to their national home in the Land of Israel. Lincoln said this was a noble dream and one shared by many Americans. The president, who was also known for his sense of humor, went on to say that his "chiropodist is a Jew, who has so many times put me upon my feet that I would have no objection to giving his countrymen a leg up." [21]

President Harry Truman was known for his toughness, as exemplified by the famous slogan, Give 'em hell, Harry! His visibly emotional moments

A Warm Heart for Israel: US President Harry Truman (L) receives a Hanukkah menorah in 1951 from Israeli Prime Minister David Ben-Gurion (R), with Israeli Ambassador to the US, Abba Eban (C).

were rare, but Israel was one topic that touched his heart. Truman biographer David McCullough reported:

"I have about three instances where Truman cried in public. They are very few and they are always real." [22]

When Chief Rabbi Yitzchak Isaac HaLevi Herzog of the newly established state of Israel came to visit President Truman in early 1949, the two had a very moving exchange, in which the Rabbi expressed his thanks to the president for his recognition of Israel. He then went on to say the following words to the president: "God put you in your mother's womb so that you could be the instrument to bring about the rebirth of Israel after almost two thousand years." Truman was visibly moved. Herzog then opened his Bible, and with the president reading along in his own Bible, the Rabbi read from the Book of Ezra (1:2), in which the Persian King Cyrus spoke the following words:

"The Lord, God of Heaven has given me all the kindness of the earth; and He has commanded me to build Him a house (Temple) at Jerusalem, which is in Judea."

On hearing these words, Truman rose from his chair and with great emotion, tears glistening in his eyes, he turned to the Chief Rabbi and asked him if his actions for the sake of the Jewish people were indeed to be interpreted thus and (that) the hand of the Almighty was in the matter. The Chief Rabbi reassured him that he had been given the task once fulfilled by the mighty King of Persia, and that he too, like Cyrus, would occupy a place of honor in the annals of the Jewish people.[23]

In 1961, then Prime Minister of Israel David Ben-Gurion, on his final trip to the US, visited former President Truman in a New York hotel suite to once again express his appreciation:

"I told him that as a foreigner, I could not judge what would be his place in American history; but his helpfulness to us, his constant sympathy with our aims in Israel, his courageous decision to recognize our new State so quickly and his steadfast support since then had given him an immortal place in Jewish history. As I said this, tears suddenly sprang to his eyes. And his eyes were still wet when he bade me good-bye. I had rarely seen anyone so moved.

"I tried to hold him for a few minutes until he had become more composed, for I recalled that the hotel corridors were full of waiting journalists and photographers. He left. A little while later, I too had to go out and a correspondent came up to me to ask, 'Why was President Truman in tears when he left you?'"[24]

Truman's emotional bonds with Israel seem to reflect a spiritual, biblical connection that transcends the usual ties of interest between nations. As the plentiful quotes from American presidents show, the dream of Israel's return to the Land after two thousand years of exile was something that was always expected in the eyes of biblically-literate people, because the prophecies clearly predicted it. Truman and so many of his predecessors were biblically bound to believe that the return to the Land was destined to happen.

The warmth of the pro-Israel Truman administration reverberated for some years, but the election of Jimmy Carter brought in a new era. As president from 1976-1980, Carter was instrumental in pushing forward the Israel-Egypt peace agreement, in which Israel gave to Egypt the vast Sinai desert, about three times the land mass of the current State of Israel, in exchange for a written peace arrangement. That deal also created a parallel framework for Palestinian autonomy, which some would say nourished the seed of what has become a very problematic Palestinian nationalism (more on that later). While one can certainly debate the merits of the arguably cold peace deal between Israel and Egypt, which nonetheless has held firm despite the ups and downs of Egyptian political stability, there is no doubt that the Jimmy Carter-Israel relationship has been all downhill since then. President Carter's last foreign policy "achievement" was his enablement, and perhaps even encouragement, of the Islamic Revolution in Iran. It can certainly be argued that Carter's halting of what had been firm political backing for the Shah of Iran was a major factor in the rise of Ayatollah Ruhollah Khomeini and his Islamic extremists to power.

When the Shah visited the White House in November 1977, he already was an embattled leader. During that visit, he was the recipient of public expressions of support from the president, but he was later chastised in private meetings by Carter for his spotty human rights record. The Shah was strongly urged to consider reaching out to dissident groups attempting to overthrow his government and "easing off" on police actions against them. This pressure was something new to the Shah and the timing of Carter's reprimand couldn't have been worse for the embattled Persian leader, who was already in a fight for both personal and political survival. Eventually, succumbing to the pressure of the revolution while simultaneously battling an advanced stage of cancer, the Shah left Iran for exile on January 16, 1979. The royal reign collapsed shortly thereafter, when guerrillas and rebel troops overwhelmed soldiers loyal to the Shah in armed street fighting. Iran voted by national referendum to become an Islamic Republic on April 1, 1979, and to approve a new democratic-theocratic hybrid constitution whereby Khomeini became Supreme Leader of the country, in December 1979. The rise to power of the Islamic ideologues in Iran almost immediately led to a flexing of muscles and a crisis with the United States, during which 52 Americans were held hostage for 444 days from November 4, 1979, to January 20, 1981, after a group of Islamic militants took over the American Embassy in Tehran in a show of support for the Iranian Revolution and anger towards "the Great Satan" ("The Little Satan" in their semantics being Israel).[25]

The Islamic theocracy has been in power in Iran ever since and has, undisputedly, been the most consistent supporter of Islamic terrorism in the Middle East and throughout the world. Furthermore, it has been quite transparent about its intention to export that revolution, not just against Israel, but against the entire free world. The weakness of President Carter in dealing with this crisis became more apparent when Ronald Reagan was elected as president in 1980. Reagan's projection of American strength caused the hostages to be quickly and unconditionally released.

In the subsequent decades after leaving office, Carter became much more vocal in his anti-Israel sentiments, calling publicly, in both writings and speeches, for the expulsion of Jews from the biblical heartland of Israel and the establishment of a Palestinian state, headed by the terrorist organizations Hamas and Fatah in its stead. These calls continued in the succeeding administrations, being echoed in various "peace plans" by Presidents George H.W. Bush, Bill Clinton, and George W. Bush. These grand plans were often negotiated discreetly, but usually were hammered out and/or unveiled at expensive American-sponsored peace summits, but what they all had in common was the "land for peace" formula, which was based on the principle of Israel's "need" to surrender land in exchange for a signed peace agreement with the Palestinians. Once the Oslo Accords were signed during the Clinton administration, the land for peace formula evolved into the internationally acclaimed goal of the two-state solution, meaning an independent Palestinian state encompassing the regions of Judea (south of Jerusalem) and Samaria (north of Jerusalem) with its capital in eastern Jerusalem, the heart of ancient, as well as present-day Israel. It didn't seem to matter to anyone that the Palestinians have been the progenitors of the art of modern Islamic terrorism, nor did it matter that they had rejected every land for peace proposal that was suggested by American presidents. The world leaders, including the respective residents of the White House, continued to propose new variations on the same failed idea.

The process of failed peace plans only speeded up during the Obama years, which saw a shift in American alliances in the Middle East and around the world. During those eight years, the Israel-United States alliance was tested and threatened like never before.

The Obama Years

"You know, I think I am the closest thing to a Jew that
has ever sat in this office. For people to say that I am
anti-Israel, or, even worse, anti-Semitic, it hurts." [1]

(Barack Obama, in White House conversation
with then Chief of Staff David Axelrod)

T he rise of Obama to the presidency was a time
of great excitement for a large segment of the
American Jewish community. As the first African-
American to be elected to the most powerful position in the
world, Obama reinforced the Jewish belief, based on the
Jewish experience in the "land of the free", that the United
States was, indeed, the country in which every individual
could achieve according to his ability and effort, rightly
unconstrained by factors such as race, religion, and gender.
It was seen by many as the fulfillment of an ideal.

However, honesty dictates that just as no individual
should be judged negatively by just race, so too, no individual
should be judged positively just by race. He or she should
be judged on factors that transcend both racism and racial
preference, factors such as achievements, worldview, and
character.

*"I have a dream that my four little children will one day live
in a nation where they will not be judged by the color of their skin,
but by the content of their character." [2]*

(Martin Luther King, Jr.)

Many liberal American Jews supported President Obama
because they liked his views on many social issues and even

his foreign policy positions, while some were conflicted about his positions on Israel and the Middle East. Surrounded by a coterie of liberal Jews, several of whom were top advisors, Obama staked positions on Israel that placed him on the Far Left of the Israeli political spectrum, and perhaps even further.

Unlike many of his predecessors, Obama didn't seem to have a natural affinity with Israel. In fact, he came to office expressing his intention to improve America's often adversarial relationship with the Islamic world, which, for the most part, was at war with Israel. Just seven years earlier, the United States had been shaken to the core by the 9-11 terrorist attack on the World Trade Center in New York City. America, under the George W. Bush administration, had, at least temporarily, become vigilant about the very real threat from what had become known as "radical Islamic terrorism". Obama saw the world differently. Having been raised as a Muslim in Indonesia by a secular, Communist mother and a Muslim stepfather, and having idolized his late father,[3] who also had been a Muslim, Obama was determined to show that the Islamic world was actually a friend of Western civilization. In his first few months in office, his very public tour of Islamic countries and televised interviews praising Islam made it clear that America's international relations had entered a new era.

"The sweetest sound I know is the Muslim call to prayer." [4]
(Barack Obama – Cairo Speech, 2009)

"The future must not belong to those who slander the prophet of Islam." [5]
(Barack Obama, speech at the United Nations 2012)

Yes, we who live near Muslim towns in Israel know very well the Muslim call to prayer. We hear it on loudspeakers from the mosque across the Shiloh valley at 4:00 a.m. every morning. To say that it disturbs our sleep would be a great understatement.

We also know that sometimes they call "*Itbach Al Yahud!*", meaning "Kill the Jews", from the loudspeakers of mosques across Israel. The sweetest sound that Obama knows.

Even before Obama was elected in 2008 for his first term, it was apparent that the theme of his campaign, change, extended in part to America's relationship with Israel. Although some American presidents have been friendlier than others, Obama was the first American president who had close alliances with avowedly anti-Israel, and anti-American, Arab-Americans. This included Rashid Khalidi, an activist and former official spokesman for WAFA – the news agency for the PLO terrorist organization. Khalidi has for many years held the Edward Said Chair of Middle East Studies at Columbia University. This anonymously-funded position (rumored to be from a Muslim donor living in the Persian Gulf) is named for the late PLO/Yasser Arafat advisor and intellectual-hater of Israel, Edward Said, formerly of Columbia University. After years of using his carefully constructed image as an oppressed, poor Palestinian who was driven from his country, in order to bash Israel in high academic and political circles, the truth about Said was finally revealed after the publication of his autobiography. There were significant parts of the book that were fabricated – in particular that he grew up as an oppressed Palestinian Arab. In reality, Said was raised in very privileged Egyptian and American homes.[6]

The extent of Barack Obama's relationship with Said is still unclear, but there is little doubt of his long-time, close relationship with Rashid Khalidi. Obama served as a paid director on the board of the Woods Fund – a Chicago-based non-profit organization – along with unrepentant ex-terrorist William Ayers. Ayers' Weather Underground terrorist group intended to overthrow the US government and took responsibility for bombings at New York City Police headquarters in 1970, the US Capitol building in 1971, and the Pentagon in 1972. [7]

> *"I don't regret setting bombs. I feel we didn't do enough."* [8]
>
> (William Ayers, September 11, 2001)

In 2001-2002, the Obama-Ayers directed Woods Fund provided two grants which totaled $75,000 for the Arab American Action Network (AAAN). This virulently anti-Israel activist group was co-founded by Khalidi – his wife even served as president. Khalidi also held an AAAN-sanctioned fundraising event for Obama's failed bid for a US House of Representatives seat in 2000. Asked several years later about Obama's role in funding the AAAN, Khalidi claimed he had never heard of the Woods Fund until it popped up on a bunch of blogs. He terminated the call when petitioned further about his links with Obama. Contacted by phone, Mona Khalidi refused to answer questions from WorldNetDaily (WND) about the AAAN's involvement with Obama. Obama's campaign headquarters did not reply to a list of questions that were sent via e-mail from the WND to the senator's press office.[9]

Three years later, an evening tribute event was held in honor of Khalidi, who was leaving Chicago for a job in New York. According to the Los Angeles Times, a special tribute came from Khalidi's friend and frequent dinner companion, the young State Sen. Barack Obama. Speaking to the crowd, Obama reminisced about meals prepared by Khalidi's wife, Mona, and conversations that had challenged his thinking. His many talks with the Khalidis, Obama said, had been "consistent reminders to me of my own blind spots and my own biases. It's for that reason that I'm hoping that, for many years to come, we continue that conversation – a conversation that is necessary not just around Mona and Rashid's dinner table, but around 'this entire world.'" [10]

These were not Obama's only questionable colleagues. They also included associates of the racist and anti-Semitic leader of the Nation of Islam, Louis Farrakhan. Obama's long time membership in a church that awarded Farrakhan with its greatest honor was also particularly troublesome.

This of course brings us to the infamous Jeremiah Wright, Obama's pastor and mentor for twenty years at that church. Wright had views that most Americans would find repulsive:

"No, no, no. Not God bless America. God damn America. That's in the Bible. For killing innocent people. God damn America for treating citizens as less than human." [11]

(Pastor Jeremiah Wright, 2003 sermon
at Trinity United Church of Christ)

Not Just "An Old Uncle" – President Obama's mentor and pastor, Jeremiah Wright, who had some very harsh words to say about America, Israel, and Jews, is seen here chatting with President Bill Clinton during a White House Prayer Breakfast in 1998.

At first, candidate Obama tried to downplay the numerous anti-American, anti-Semitic and racist statements made by Reverend Wright. Obama said that Rev. Wright "is like an old uncle who says things I don't always agree with." He tried to further downplay the statements by telling a Jewish group that everyone has someone like Rev. Wright in their family.[12] Once it became evident that this answer wasn't going to satisfy people who had read the shocking quotes, seen the videos, and realized that Obama considered Pastor Wright to be his mentor, the campaign shifted into damage control mode. Obama resigned from his church and repudiated the statements of the pastor who had married him, had baptized his daughters, and had been the inspiration for the title of Obama's book, *The Audacity of Hope*. The most troubling part of this whole affair was that despite the many problematic videos which surfaced during the campaign and Wright's reputation that was well known in his community and beyond, Obama still insisted that in the twenty years that he had attended the church, he had never heard any of these controversial speeches.[13]

During the 2008 election campaign, there were warning signs for all supporters of a strong Israel-US relationship, yet paradoxically, the liberal Jewish community proved that its liberal ideology and knee-jerk rejection of Republicans was more enduring than its attachment to Israel. Obama managed to keep the support of American Jews and eventually won 78% of their votes.[14] Nonetheless, in an attempt to maintain and expand on his already strong Jewish support, Obama spoke positively about the relationship between the US and Israel right up until Election Day, but his focus abruptly shifted after taking office. His emphasis became America's relationship with the Islamic world. In fact, it was almost an obsession.

In a July 2010 interview, NASA Administrator Charles

Ordered By Obama to Make Muslims Feel Good: NASA Chief Charles Bolden was given strange instructions by President Obama.

Bolden, revealed the bizarre mission that had recently been entrusted to him by President Obama. NASA – National Aeronautical Space Agency – is the governmental body which is responsible for exploring new frontiers in outer space, sending astronauts to the moon, building rockets, spaceships and space stations for scientific research, and planning flights to other planets to advance human knowledge. Suddenly, NASA was given a new high priority mission, assigned to its chief administrator by President Obama:

"When I became the NASA administrator – or before I became the NASA administrator – he charged me with three things. One was he wanted me to help re-inspire children to want to get into science and math, he wanted me to expand our international relationships, and third, and perhaps foremost, he wanted me to find a way to reach out to the Muslim world and engage much more with dominantly Muslim nations to help them feel good about their historic contribution to science ... and math and engineering." [15]

Given the Muslim world's almost universal political and economic boycott of Israel, as well as its support for the Islamic terrorist organizations that have always made Israel their primary target, the sharp turn towards the Islamic world included a shifting of alliances away from Israel.

The Obama years were noted for the unyielding pressure on Israel to freeze Jewish building of homes in, and eventually to surrender Judea and Samaria (the West Bank), its historic heartland, and parts of Jerusalem, its capital city, all land Israel had recaptured in a defensive war, the Six Day War of 1967. The conflicts peaked during a very uncomfortable visit to the White House in March of 2010, during which Obama and Israeli Prime Minister Benjamin Netanyahu went head to head over the issue of Israeli building permits in Judea, Samaria, and Jerusalem. At a particularly tense late afternoon meeting with Obama, during which the two clashed repeatedly over Israeli construction in eastern Jerusalem, Obama abruptly stormed out, saying that he was "going to the residential wing to have dinner with Michelle and the girls." Netanyahu and his entourage were left alone to fend for their dinner. [16]

The tone of the US-Israel relationship soured further when the Obama administration sought to send subtle – and not-so-subtle – signals of cooperation to the Muslim world at Israel's expense. This included the White House-released photograph of President Obama speaking to Netanyahu during Obama's first year in office. In the photograph, Obama has his legs on his desk with the soles of his shoes clearly facing the camera.

In Arabic culture, this is a clear sign of insult and it is considered rude even to display the sole of one's shoe to another person. It seems unlikely that Obama could have so easily forgotten about the infamous "shoe attack" on President George W. Bush in December of 2008 when an Iraqi television journalist hurled two shoes at President Bush, who was holding a joint news conference with Iraqi Prime Minister Nouri al Maliki to mark the signing of a US-Iraq security agreement. The journalist responsible for the violent political protest, Muthathar al Zaidi, tossed his shoes at Bush

A Shoe For Israel, A Message for the Islamic World: President Obama speaks to Prime Minister Netanyahu in this White House released photo, as heavy pressure is applied on Israel to halt all building in its heartland communities, including Jerusalem. Were the figurative shoe soles in the Israeli face an intentional message to the Muslim world?

and yelled, "This is a goodbye kiss, you dog". Furthermore, President George W. Bush's national security adviser and subsequent secretary of state, Condoleezza Rice was referred to by the particularly insulting first name Kundara – meaning shoe – in many Arab circles.[17]

Another example of how the Obama administration sent subtle messages to the Arab and Muslim world about Israel occurred with Secretary of State Hillary Clinton's publicized telephone berating of Netanyahu. The Jerusalem municipality announced that the Israeli government had approved a building project in a northern Jerusalem neighborhood. According to Clinton's spokesman, this announcement, which came during Vice President Joseph Biden's visit to Israel, supposedly embarrassed the vice president, and "frustrated" Clinton. Netanyahu almost immediately

An Insincere Smile? US Secretary of State Hillary Clinton with Israeli Prime Minister Bibi Netanyahu at the King David Hotel in Jerusalem, 2009. Clinton was a frequent critic of Israel's granting of building permits to Jews in Jerusalem, which King David established as Israel's capital city over three thousand years ago.

apologized to Biden for the perceived insensitivity.[18]

Nonetheless, the altercation revealed more about the Obama administration's insensitivity to Israel's most basic concerns. If there is one issue that unites almost all Jewish Israelis, as well as Israel's friends around the world, it is the right of the Jewish state to build in its capital city, Jerusalem, which has been the capital of Israel for over three thousand years. The reigns of King David and King Solomon, during which time the Holy Temple was built on Mt. Moriah in the Old City of Jerusalem, resonates as the peak of Israel's sovereignty in the land. From the time of the destruction of Jerusalem and the Temple by the Romans almost two thousand years ago, all Jews around the world have prayed facing Jerusalem and specifically, the Temple Mount.[19] Every year at the Passover Seder (Passover's festive and educational meal), Jews loudly proclaim, "Next year in the rebuilt Jerusalem!"

President Obama, along with his surrogates like Hillary Clinton, and her successor John Kerry, who in late December 2016, vehemently and publicly condemned Israel "settlements" at the United Nations,[20] repeatedly showed a profound lack of concern or respect for the overwhelming majority of Israelis who support an undivided Jerusalem under Israel's sovereignty.

The heart and soul of the Jew has always yearned for the land of Zion and its capital city, Jerusalem. Whether berating the Israeli Prime Minister by putting a symbolic shoe in his face or denying Israel's sovereignty in Jerusalem, the tone of the Obama administration was undoubtedly the most hostile that Israel has been confronted with.

The tensions in tone were echoed in both policy and action. Israel experienced eight years of intense pressure to freeze the building of Jewish homes in Judea, Samaria, and Jerusalem. Simultaneously, Obama, Clinton, and Kerry all engaged in the obscene equating of such building with the encouragement and financing of terrorism by the Palestinian Authority, as if to say that a fair deal would be for Israel to prevent Jews from building or expanding their homes and in exchange, the PA would stop paying the terrorist murderers of Jewish families and encouraging such attacks.

The evolution over time and administrations of American pressure on Israel was apparent. While President George W. Bush had referred to the rebuilt Jewish communities in Judea, Samaria, and Jerusalem as an obstacle in the way of successful peace negotiations, Obama went head-to-head with Israel Prime Minister Benjamin Netanyahu in order to choke off all growth in the Jewish biblical heartland communities.

"I will talk about Israeli settlement expansion, about how that is, that can be, you know, an impediment to success." [21]

(President George W. Bush)

"The United States does not accept the legitimacy of continued Israeli settlements.... It is time for these settlements to stop." [22]
(President Barack Obama's Cairo, Egypt speech, June 4, 2009)

"We want to see a stop to settlement construction, additions, natural growth – any kind of (Jewish) settlement activity. That is what the president has called for." [23]
(Secretary of State Hillary Clinton, Al-Jazeera, May 19, 2009)

Eventually, Netanyahu caved in to the pressure and the result was a unilateral ten months freeze on all Jewish building in Judea, Samaria, and Jerusalem, ostensibly in order to coax the Palestinians back to the negotiating table. Like any good poker player, PA leader Mahmoud Abbas pocketed the concrete gain and ignored any implied obligation on his part.

During Obama's last month in office, he approved, and, working together with his Secretary of State John Kerry, actually orchestrated the American abstention in the UN Security Council resolution condemning "Israeli settlement building", thus, without an American veto, enabling it to be unanimously approved. According to transcripts released by Egyptian daily Al-Youm Al-Saba'a, Kerry along with US National Security Adviser Susan Rice, met with Secretary General of the PLO Executive Committee Saeb Erekat and Majed Faraj, head of the Palestinian Authority's General Intelligence Service to plan cooperation in pushing through the resolution.[24]

Whether Obama saw that resolution as a last shoe in the face of Israel, we may never know. What is clear, however, is that Israel got the message loud and clear. A 2016 survey showed that Jewish Israelis ranked Barack Obama as the "worst" US president in relation to Israel in the last thirty years – 63% of Israelis put Obama in the "worst" category, while 16% rated Jimmy Carter as the second "worst" president. [25]

Looking back in retrospect at the eight difficult years of Obama, it's clear that a large majority of Israelis looked eagerly to the American elections for a changing of the guard in Washington. Interestingly, Obama was never perceived as a friend, nor as an ally, by most Israelis, including those on the Left. The same couldn't be said of his predecessor and fellow Democrat, President Bill Clinton. While it can be said that Clinton shared Obama's pro-Palestinian state views, and he did pressure Israel in some very contentious meetings, he was never perceived by the average Israeli as being anti-Israel. Ever the charmer, and knowing how to play the Israeli crowd, Clinton caressed the Israeli populace with his friendly smile and occasional use of a Hebrew word or two. Obama, despite his verbal skills and charisma, failed miserably in that respect, as it was always clear that his emotional affinity was with the Muslim world and that he viewed Israel, at best, as a terrible annoyance to his worldview. That is how most Israelis will remember him.

Chapter Three
A Campaign Like No Other

"Every great political campaign rewrites the rules; devising a new way to win is what gives campaigns a comparative advantage against their foes." [1]

(John Podhoretz)

After the tense Obama years, Israelis had high hopes that the 2016 elections would bring an improvement in the relationship with its closest ally. The word on the Israeli street was "anything is better than Obama". While former Secretary of State Hillary Clinton didn't have her husband's warmth and remarkable ability to emphasize the positive, she wasn't perceived as being anti-Israel like Obama.

Clinton's main competitor in the Democratic race was Senator Bernie Sanders of Vermont, a Jewish man originally from Brooklyn, with an accent and intonation to match. Bernie had the distinction of volunteering for a few months in the mid-1960s in an Israeli kibbutz of the leftist Zionist Hashomer Hatzair movement. Sanders had been reticent during the campaign regarding matters of his Jewish upbringing and especially his time in Israel, where he traveled with his first wife, Deborah Shiling, who also was Jewish (His second and current wife is not Jewish). The Sanders campaign turned away queries about his Israel stay and the candidate himself seemed to avoid the topic.[2]

Much of Sanders' reluctance to discuss his Jewish background may have derived from a desire not to alienate his core followers. In recent years, the Far Left of the Democratic Party has gained prominence, with the rise of such polarizing

Declaring Loyalty to the Book of Jihad? US Rep. Keith Ellison (D-MN) takes his oath of office with hand on Thomas Jefferson's Koran during swearing-in ceremony, with Speaker of the House Nancy Pelosi and his wife Kim at the US Capitol. While Ellison praised Jefferson's openness to "wisdom from a variety of sources", left unsaid was the fact that the former president had purchased a Koran to understand the Jihadist mentality of the Muslim Barbary Pirates, that had been terrorizing American ships at sea.

figures as Congressman Keith Ellison, the Deputy Chair of the Democratic National Committee. Aside from being a Muslim, who, with the help of House Minority Leader Nancy Pelosi took his oath of office on a Koran, Ellison spoke at the convention of the Islamic Society of North America, which is part of the CAIR-Hamas network, at least according to the Fifth Circuit Court of Appeals, which found that "the government has produced ample evidence to establish the associations of CAIR, ISNA, NAIT, with the Islamic Association for Palestine, and with Hamas" during the Holy Land Foundation case. All of these organizations were proven to have been involved in and/or supported Islamic terrorism. Furthermore, Ellison went on a pilgrimage to Mecca sponsored by the Muslim American Society, which is simply the Muslim Brotherhood under another name. In Mecca, he met with Sheikh Abdallah Bin Bayyah, an officer of a Muslim Brotherhood group that issued a fatwa against US troops in Iraq and supported Palestinian terrorists in Israel.[3]

Despite his Jewish background, or maybe because of it, Sanders was always looking over his shoulder at his anti-Israel supporters and allies. Therefore, it wasn't a great surprise when he made statements and supported actions that would serve to harm Israel, since that is one way to appease the Far Left. Sanders named three prominent critics of Israel to the committee charged with formulating the Democratic Party platform: Rep. Ellison; James Zogby, the president of the Arab American Institute, and Cornel West, a philosopher and supporter of the anti-Israel Boycott, Divestment and Sanctions movement.[4]

With the leadership of Jewish politicians like Sanders, it has become acceptable for Democrats to support boycott movements against Israel, to provide political backing for Mahmoud Abbas and the Palestinian terrorist organizations

Jewish Boy From Brooklyn Panders to Anti-Israel Left: Democratic Presidential Candidate Bernie Sanders, a self-proclaimed Socialist, supported actions/individuals that were harmful to Israel, since that is one way to appease the Far Left.

that comprise the Palestinian Authority, and to criticize the right of young Jewish families to build "settlements", which really means homes and neighborhoods, in Israel's historic heartland of Judea, Samaria, and Jerusalem.

While much attention was focused during the campaign on the rivalry between Sanders' left flank and Clinton's "moderate" faction, when it came to Israel, the differences weren't so great. In their debates, speeches, and, of course, their past statements and voting records, Clinton and Sanders have both voiced strong opposition to Israeli sovereignty, and specifically, "settlements", including building in Jerusalem. Both strongly supported the reckless Iran nuclear deal that was opposed by most Israelis across the political spectrum.[5]

Furthermore, as noted earlier, Clinton, as Secretary of State was notorious for her telephone berating of Netanyahu after the Jerusalem municipal planning committee granted building permits for 900 apartments in northern Jerusalem. The meeting of the committee, scheduled well in advance to decide on the permits, happened to fall during Vice President Joe Biden's visit to Israel.[6]

But it wasn't just the unpleasant phone call altercation that revealed the problematic nature of Hillary's dealings with Israel, which reflected the Obama administration's overall attitude towards the Jewish state. There was also the issue of the Clinton Foundation and its funding by several Islamic nations that are in a state of war with Israel. The ongoing FBI investigations may or may not reveal if Hillary's close ties with the Muslim nations that supported the Clinton Foundation were part of illegal pay-to-play schemes that influenced her arrogant tone toward Israel and her decisions as Secretary of State, but her apparent lack of respect for the positions of Israel's elected leadership didn't win her the affection of the Israeli populace.

The Republicans, however, presented a contrasting picture. The initial complete field of seventeen candidates was led by Senator Ted Cruz, who officially kicked off the Republican presidential primary on March 23, 2015, by entering the race.

"I believe in the power of millions of courageous conservatives rising up to reignite the promise of America."
(Ted Cruz, in a speech to students
at the Christian evangelical Liberty University.)

Cruz also made a clear statement about America's relationship with the promised land and its people, to which he received a rousing standing ovation, thereby showing that supporting Israel had become a key issue in the GOP:

"Instead of a president who boycotts Prime Minister Netanyahu,

Non-Politician, Master Campaigner: Donald Trump, seen here debating Sen. Ted Cruz (R-TX), methodically eliminated seventeen distinguished GOP candidates in 2016, defying the predictions of most political pundits.

imagine a president who stands unapologetically with the nation of Israel." [7]

Cruz eventually dropped out of the race, after getting the support of millions of voters – many of them conservative – but not quite enough to win it. The next day, John Kasich dropped out, too, leaving just one candidate in the GOP field: presumptive nominee Donald Trump, who had entered the race on June 16, 2015.

In between Cruz's initial speech and Kasich's departure, fourteen other candidates entered and exited the GOP race.[8] It was a wild campaign, with a wide field of talented, experienced public servants. These included political heavyweights, such as initial frontrunner Florida Governor Jeb Bush, Wisconsin Governor Scott Walker, Florida Senator Marco Rubio, Kentucky Senator Rand Paul, former Texas Governor Rick Perry, and former Arkansas Governor Mike

Huckabee, along with respected newcomers Dr. Ben Carson and businesswoman Carly Fiorina.

Like Father Like Son: Donald Trump learned from father, Fred Trump, the values of hard work, frugality, and having a vision for success.

Trump came to the campaign as an extremely successful businessman, having built a virtual empire of Trump-labeled buildings in New York City. Trump had grown up in the outer borough of Queens in a relatively modest home. Nonetheless, his father Fred was a successful builder himself, having changed the face of Brooklyn and Queens with thousands of homes for the middle class in plain but sturdy brick rental towers, clustered together in immaculately groomed parks.

Fred Trump, a self-made man, built more than 27,000 apartments and row houses in the neighborhoods of Coney Island, Bensonhurst, Sheepshead Bay, Flatbush, and Brighton Beach in Brooklyn and Flushing and Jamaica Estates in Queens. Mr. Trump didn't believe in displays of wealth – with one exception. For decades, he insisted on a Cadillac, always navy blue, always gleaming, and always replaced every three years, its "FCT" license plate announcing its owner wherever he went.

He was a frugal man. According to his sons, he would routinely drive his Cadillac to one of his many construction sites after the day's work was over. Wearing a natty suit – with his chiseled features and wide grin, he resembled a silent-film star – he would walk through the studs and across the plywood floors, picking up unused nails to hand back to his carpenters the next day.[9]

A Vision of Modest Housing: Trump Village in Brooklyn represented Fred Trump's vision of middle and lower middle-class housing in the outer New York City boroughs. Donald learned from his father the importance of having a goal and doing everything necessary to achieve it. He then took it to the next level with his luxury projects in Manhattan and elsewhere, but the value of having a vision and working hard to achieve it remained the same.

His son Donald clearly learned at the feet of his father the value of hard work and conservative economics, but he also learned what it means to have a vision and to follow that vision with goals that are both great and practical at the same time.

In the mid-1970s, Fred Trump lent his support – and a small amount of money – to his son Donald's aspirations of becoming a developer. According to Donald's younger brother Robert, "But what he lent was mostly knowledge; Donald really did it on his own, along with whatever boost he got from being Fred Trump's son, of course." [10]

Fred Trump gave one million dollars in trusts to each of his children and grandchildren, but even if he actually gave more in loans or in other forms, as has been reported in some media, there is no doubt that Donald Trump was enormously successful and used his inheritance to create a real estate empire worth billions of dollars.[11]

Looking back, Donald said he was happy that his father stuck to Brooklyn and Queens. "It was good for me ... you know, being the son of somebody, it could have been competition to me. This way, I got Manhattan all to myself!"[12]

After years of toying with the idea and teasing the media about it, Donald Trump the builder, decided to become Donald Trump the politician by throwing his very large hat into the presidential race. Despite his lack of political experience, and maybe even because of it, Trump managed to set himself apart and above the crowded field. From the beginning of the first raucous debate and onward, he used an attention-getting street-savvy style and announced an assortment of bold policy proposals to battle America's enemies, along with a lot of aggressive criticisms and name-calling of his confused opponents, who often seemed not to know what had hit them. Some examples:

"ISIS is taking over a lot of the oil and certain areas of Iraq. And I said you take away their wealth, that you go and knock the hell out of the oil, take back the oil. We take over the oil, which we should have done in the first place." [13]

(Trump on Meet the Press, August 16, 2015)

"Weak and low energy @JebBush, whose campaign is a disaster, is now doing ads against me where he tries to look like a tough guy." [14]

(Trump on Twitter December 22, 2015)

"I will build a great wall – and nobody builds walls better than me, believe me – and I'll build them very inexpensively. I will build a great, great wall on our southern border, and I will make Mexico pay for that wall." [15]

(Trump, June 2015)

After Trump had torn down the seemingly invincible Jeb Bush's front-runner machine, then methodically doing the same with Carson, Rubio, and Cruz, Trump became the front-runner, although at first, distinguishing himself on the important topic of Israel wasn't so easy.

Cruz, Huckabee, and Rubio already had a strong following among pro-Israel Republicans.

In the past thirty years, Israel has become a significant litmus-test issue in the GOP and it's become critical for any candidacy, not just to say that you are pro-Israel, but to show that you really stand with Israel on the critical issues that have been in dispute – rebuilding Israeli sovereignty in Jerusalem, Judea, and Samaria, fighting Islamic terrorism, and combatting Iran. In many ways, the evangelical Christian population has become the main faction in the GOP pushing for Israel as a key issue in the party. Some 26% of the electorate identified in the 2016 elections as born-again or evangelical Christian, and 81% of them voted for Trump over Clinton. Capturing evangelical support is essential for

Republican candidates; as of 2014, evangelical and born-again voters represented the plurality (45%) of voters who are Republican or who lean Republican.[16]

That populace has taken a strong stand against any division of the Land of Israel, has supported the recognition of Jerusalem as Israel's eternal capital, and has vehemently backed Israel's opposition to the Iran nuclear deal, which was signed by the Obama administration, and which put billions of dollars into the hands of Iran's mullahs. Those funds are being used to finance terrorism around the world, and to further what the Ayatollah Ruhollah Khomeini called "exporting the Islamic Revolution".[17]

As the campaign progressed, it was clear that the evangelicals were a population that could not be ignored, and for most of them, standing with Israel was a no-brainer.

An event that could not be ignored was the March 2016 AIPAC Policy Conference in Washington, DC, attended by thousands of American Jews, and, more recently, many Christian Zionists as well. The America Israel Political Action Committee is a major lobbying organization that supports legislation that strengthens the US-Israel relationship. In an election year, this event is considered a "must" appearance for every serious candidate to pledge support for Israel. It would not be Donald Trump's first time speaking to a predominantly Jewish audience, but as the front-runner, his appearance at this event was highly anticipated, both by his critics and by potential supporters.

Two Reform (the very liberal stream of Judaism) rabbis, David Paskin and Jesse Olitzky, organized a small, but very visible protest, calling it "Come Together Against Hate", apparently alluding to the AIPAC conference's motto "Come Together", but the protesters had a different message:

"We denounce in the strongest possible terms the bigotry, racism,

xenophobia, and misogyny expressed by Mr. Trump, and violence promoted by him, at various points throughout his campaign. We refuse to stand idly by and let his hateful message become a part of the AIPAC Policy Conference." [18]

(From a press release of the rabbis
posted on a specially created website)

The people marching along Washington's streets waved Palestinian flags and carried banners, with various slogans, calling to "Boycott Israel", "Free Palestine", "Stop Genocide of Palestine" and other not so Israel-friendly slogans. Being that at least some of the protesters were Jews, several of whom called themselves rabbis, the blatantly anti-Israel message was repugnant to most of the conference attendees, who, while expressing a wide variety of political views, were there to support a strong US-Israel relationship, not to preach the hateful slogans of Israel's enemies.[19]

Meanwhile, inside the hall, Donald Trump was receiving rousing ovations, not for empty slogans, but for staking out concrete policy positions that the attendees seemed to agree with, as well as saying some unconventional things that apparently needed to be expressed. An estimated 300 of the approximately 18,000 attendees walked out, but everyone else stayed and most listened, either respectfully or enthusiastically. Several highlights:

- *On Iran:* "The problem is that they can keep the terms and get the bombs by simply running out the clock, and of course they'll keep the billions and billions of dollars that we so stupidly and foolishly gave them," Trump said. "When the restrictions expire, Iran will have an industrial-size nuclear capability ready to go." [20]

- *On Jerusalem:* "We will move the American embassy to

the eternal capital of the Jewish people," he declared to applause. "We will send a clear signal that there is no daylight between America and our most reliable ally, the State of Israel." [21]

- *On the UN:* "An agreement imposed by the United Nations would be a total and complete disaster," he predicted. "The US must oppose this resolution and use the power of our veto, which I will use as president, 100%." [22]

- *On the Peace Process:* Imposing an external solution "will only further delegitimize Israel. It will be a disaster and a catastrophe for Israel" and "reward Palestinian terrorism." [23]

The AIPAC Policy Conference proved to be a boost for the Trump campaign's pro-Israel credentials. Combined with his strong economy credentials and his policy positions on combatting ISIS and other Islamic terrorism, as well as fighting illegal immigration, Trump went on to win the GOP nomination.

In one of his first acts as the undisputed GOP candidate, he named Indiana Governor Mike Pence as his running mate. Pence, known to be a deeply religious Christian, has long been a friend of Israel and a believer in the biblical mandate to stand with Israel. Just as it was for Presidents Washington, Adams, Lincoln, and Truman, along with so many other biblically-literate Americans, Pence's bond with Israel is a bond that comes from both the head and the heart. He loves Israel because he loves America's biblical heritage, not just because he loves freedom and democracy. He loves America because he loves the Judeo-Christian civilization on which it was founded. Just as House Minority Leader Nancy Pelosi and Senate Minority Leader Chuck Schumer's political views are based on their own liberal value systems, Pence's political beliefs have been derived from his religious values and that's certainly not something that he needs to be ashamed of, even if much of the mainstream media tells him that he should be. He is actually in very good company, as the Founding Fathers would attest to, and there is certainly a commonality in a political values system based on the biblical roots:

"So great is my veneration for the Bible, that the earlier my children begin to read it the more confident will be my hopes that they will prove useful citizens to their country and respectable members of society." [24]

(John Quincy Adams)

"The Hebrews have done more to civilize men than any other nation. If I were an atheist, and believed blind eternal fate, I should still believe that fate had ordained the Jews to be the most essential instrument for civilizing the nations." [25]

(John Quincy Adams)

"More than anything else, let me be clear – we need to be willing to fight for freedom, and free markets, and traditional moral values. That's what the American people want to see this movement and this party return to." [26]

(Mike Pence)

"I never thought I'd live to see the day that an American administration would denounce the state of Israel for rebuilding Jerusalem." [27]

(Mike Pence)

For Mike Pence, belief in God and Bible, support for freedom, support for family values, and support for Israel are inseparable. It is probably for that reason that Trump selected him. Despite the lies of the slanderers on the left who have publicly and aggressively questioned his intelligence, Donald Trump is a very smart guy who made a very smart choice. No one creates the financial empire that he did without having brains, and very good ones at that.

Given Trump's three marriages, one very public affair, and two messy divorces that were featured in all the tabloids, as well as his shoot from the hip style, Trump needed to be complemented by an unquestionably moral, modest, and humble individual, but one with a lot of talent. Governor Mike Pence fit the bill perfectly, and Trump had the wisdom and people skills to recognize that they would make a good team.

While we're on that topic, the family values issue is a particularly important one that haunted Trump throughout the campaign, and it certainly could be said that some of the criticism was justified when speaking about his marital stability at times. Nonetheless, as Hillary Clinton alluded to in one of the debates when she was forced to say something positive about her opponent, and as his ex-wife Ivana has confirmed, Trump was a very good father, a fact that is

Raising Children Together: Despite the challenge of raising rich kids in a high profile marriage that eventually failed, Donald and Ivana Trump worked together to raise hard-working children with strong family values.

evident in his grown children. It's not easy raising rich kids, and especially with all the public soap opera media madness and the intense business climate that was always going on around them. Donald and Ivana Trump were successful business people, but more importantly, were successful parents, and even though Ivana had custody after the divorce, they cooperated post-divorce, as well. This passage, from an article written by Maggie Gallagher, who apparently, did not support Trump during the primary campaign, and possibly not even after, is especially instructive about the real character of Donald Trump:

"It is true that Trump has discarded two wives, cheated on at least one of them, and (as I have) made a child out of wedlock. But he then married the woman who bore that child, however briefly. He has always supported all of his children financially, unlike many unmarried or irregularly married fathers. And he has managed to create and maintain close relationships with those children despite the barriers to fatherhood imposed by divorce. They, in turn, are the best part of Donald J. Trump: educated, hardworking, productive, and (in the case of Ivana's kids, at least) all married with children themselves. Ivana Trump deserves the lion's share of credit for raising her three impressive older children with Trump, since she had full custody after the divorce. But she gives him credit for having her back along the way."

"If I would say 'no' to the kids, they would go to their father and say, 'Daddy, Daddy can we get that and that ...?' And he would ask, 'What did mother say?' They would tell him, 'Mommy said no,' so that meant 'no.'"

"One can hardly ask for anything better from a multiply-divorced dad, and it is clear it did not happen by accident. Trump really does seem to understand that many things matter more than making money."

"What he chose to say after his first great political victory in New Hampshire was telling. He began by thanking his family – not generically, but in great detail. First, he thanked his dead parents. Then, he moved on to his sisters. And finally, on a night where Trump could've been forgiven for indulging his own outsize ego, he instead took a moment to recall his dead older brother Fred..."

"I want to thank my brother, my late brother, Fred, what a fantastic guy. I learned so much from Fred. Taught me more than just about anybody. Just probably about even with my father, a fantastic guy. So, I want to thank Fred. He's up there and he's looking down also."

"Fred Trump, Jr. died of alcoholism in 1981. In 1999, when Trump's father, Fred, Sr., died, Fred Jr.'s children were the only grandchildren cut out of the will. Yet in "The Art of the Deal", Trump spoke with great love about his older brother, who disappointed their father by refusing to enter the family business, instead choosing to follow his passion and become a pilot. Trump learned from his brother two great things: 1) Substance abuse destroys lives; and 2) making money isn't the main definition of success; real success is love."

"That's what he told Wisconsin college students a few weeks ago..."

"You have to absolutely love what you do, ideally love what you do in a good business ... But you know what ... the loving is more important than having that good business ... To me, a successful person has a great family who loves the family, loves the children and the children love him or her. To me, that's a much more successful person than a person that's made a million dollars or 10 million dollars and is miserable and doesn't have a good family and nobody likes the person. I've seen 'em. I think I've seen every type of person there is that God created, if you want to know the truth, and the people that are the happiest are not necessarily the people that are the wealthiest." [28]

In short, Donald Trump is not the monster that some networks would have you believe, even if his style could often be more refined and his statements more eloquent, but it's hard for the objective observer not to agree with the sentiments expressed above.

Nonetheless, the fierce campaign of character assassination against him picked up steam as the election campaign moved into the fall season of Trump-Clinton debates. There was the revelation of the Access Hollywood tape, the secretly recorded lewd conversation from 2005 between Trump and co-anchor Billy Bush, which was terrible, but which was, nonetheless, only crude locker room talk, as opposed to the very credible allegations of former President Bill Clinton's multiple affairs, even with subordinates while in political office, and his wife Hillary's complicity in attacking the women who went public with their charges against the former president. In a public statement, Trump admitted his shortcomings, while pointing out to the public that the former president had done far worse:

"This was locker room banter, a private conversation that took place many years ago. Bill Clinton has said far worse to me on the golf course – not even close. I apologize if anyone was offended. I've never said I'm a perfect person, nor pretended to be someone that I'm not. I've said and done things I regret, and the words released today on this more than a decade-old video are one of them. Anyone who knows me knows these words don't reflect who I am. I said it, I was wrong, and I apologize..." [29]

Trump continued:

"Let's be honest: We're living in the real world. This is nothing

more than a distraction from the important issues we're facing today. We are losing our jobs, we're less safe than we were eight years ago, and Washington is totally broken. Hillary Clinton and her kind have run our country into the ground. I've said some foolish things, but there's a big difference between the words and actions of other people. Bill Clinton has actually abused women, and Hillary has bullied, attacked, shamed and intimidated his victims." [30]

The fact that Hillary was Trump's opponent actually reduced the lasting impact of an issue that could have destroyed his campaign. The focus soon returned to the issues facing the country and when the character issue returned with the Clinton Foundation scandal and Hillary's email scandal, her honesty and integrity on the job came into doubt in a big way. Many questions needed to be asked about the Clinton Foundation's long list of foreign government donors and potential pay-to-play schemes. Ten of millions of dollars were accepted from countries like Saudi Arabia, Oman, United Arab Emirates, Kuwait, Qatar, Brunei, and Algeria. Many of these donations were given during Hillary's term as Secretary of State. [31]

Can it be that these foreign governments were giving due to their own altruistic concern for the Clinton Foundation's supposed good works in depressed countries like Haiti? What were those Arab countries promised in exchange for their huge donations? How did all of this influence Clinton's attitudes towards Israel and the Middle East, including ingenuously blaming the fatal attack on the American Embassy in Benghazi, Libya on an obscure, virtually unknown, amateur video critical of Islam?

Since 2016, the FBI has taken on the challenge of delving into these and other related questions by investigating not only potential political corruption on a major scale, but also its malignant influence on international affairs.

Hopefully, the truth will be revealed.

The Trump-Clinton debates were intense and actually were mainly focused on the issues facing the United States, among them the economy, illegal immigration, and the Iran nuclear deal, which Trump blasted and Clinton defended. The Iran deal issue was a recurring bone of contention on the campaign trail, with the opponents expressing sharply contrasting views of the deal's ability to stop Iran from getting the nuclear bomb, as well as the weapons to go with it. Some highlights from the candidates:

Clinton: *"The understanding that the major world powers have reached with Iran is an important step toward a comprehensive agreement that would prevent Iran from getting a nuclear weapon and strengthen the security of the United States, Israel, and the region. The President (Barack Obama) and Secretary (of State John) Kerry have been persistent and determined in pursuit of this goal, building on a decade of bipartisan pressure and diplomacy."* [32]
(Hillary Clinton, April 2015)

"I also welcome the full implementation of the nuclear agreement, an important achievement of diplomacy backed by pressure. Implementation marks an important step forward in preventing Iran from obtaining a nuclear weapon. Iran has dismantled centrifuges, disabled a reactor, and shipped out almost all of its enriched uranium. These are important steps that make the United States, our allies, and the entire world safer. I congratulate President Obama and his team, and I'm proud of the role I played to get this process started." [33]
(Hillary Clinton, January 2016 – after the agreement was finalized)

Trump: *"My number one priority is to dismantle the disastrous deal with Iran. I have been in business a long time. I know deal-making and let me tell you, this deal is catastrophic – for America, for Israel, and for the whole Middle East. The problem here is* *fundamental. We have rewarded the world's leading state sponsor of terror with $150 billion and we received absolutely nothing in return. I've studied this issue in greater detail than almost anybody. The biggest concern with the deal is not necessarily that Iran is going to violate it, although it already has, the bigger problem is that they can keep the terms and still get to the bomb by simply running out the clock, and, of course, they keep the billions. The deal doesn't even require Iran to dismantle its military nuclear capability! Yes, it places limits on its military nuclear program for only a certain number of years. But when those restrictions expire, Iran will have an industrial-size military nuclear capability ready to go, and with zero provision for delay, no matter how bad Iran's behavior is.*

When I am president, I will adopt a strategy that focuses on three things when it comes to Iran:

- *First, we will stand up to Iran's aggressive push to destabilize and dominate the region. Iran is a very big problem and will continue to be, but if I'm elected president, I know how to deal with trouble.*

- *Secondly, we will totally dismantle Iran's global terror network. Iran has seeded terror groups all over the world. During the last five years, Iran has perpetrated terror attacks in twenty-five different countries on five continents. They've got terror cells everywhere, including in the western hemisphere very close to home. Iran is the biggest sponsor of terrorism around the world and we will work to dismantle that reach.*

- *Third, at the very least, we must hold Iran accountable by restructuring the terms of the previous deal. Iran has already – since the deal is in place – test-fired ballistic missiles three times. Those ballistic missiles, with a range of 1,250 miles, were designed to intimidate not only Israel, which is only 600 miles away but also intended to frighten Europe, and, someday, the United States." [34]*

(Donald J. Trump, March 2016)

Iran's leadership has coined the United States "the Big Satan" and Israel "the Little Satan", so what did little Israel think of the deal? Being the primary target of Iran, even though the United States isn't too far behind, it is instructive to hear what Israel's reaction was to the deal. Israeli politics can be quite intense and polarizing, with sharp differences of opinion between the Right and the Left on many issues, but unlike the United States, where the Democrats, with several notable exceptions, voted for the agreement, in Israel, it was different.

On the issue of the Iran deal, there was an almost universal political consensus against the agreement. In Israel, a tiny country about the size of New Jersey, surrounded by mostly hostile Arab Muslim nations with a land mass more than 700 times greater, we can't afford to take chances like the Iran deal. No one trusts the leadership of Iran and no one trusts an agreement that will allow the radical Muslims that rule Iran to, at least partially, continue their nuclear research program with the goal of achieving nuclear breakout capability shortly after the agreement expires.

When there is an existential threat, all Israelis unite, and Iran is seen by the entire political spectrum as such an existential threat, while the deal wasn't seen as halting that threat. Across the Israeli political spectrum, the reaction was similar. A day after the agreement was signed, a poll conducted by Israel's Channel 10 found that an overwhelming 69% of Israelis opposed it, while only 10% were in favor, with 21% undecided. Even more revealing of the Israeli perspective, when asked whether they thought the agreement would prevent Iran from achieving nuclear capabilities, 74% said it wouldn't, while only 10% said it would, with 16% undecided.[35]

On the issues of the peace process and settlements, candidate Trump took more of a wait and see position, making it clear that he was going to be in learning mode on the issue, which actually was a breath of fresh air. Rather than spouting the usual mantras of "land for peace" and the "two state solution", Trump seemed reluctant to get into details, often referring questioners to the Co-Chairmen of his Israel Advisory Committee, Jason Greenblatt and David Friedman. Both were long-standing lawyers for the Trump organization, whose judgment on Israel-related issues, and in general, were greatly respected by the candidate.

In addition, Greenblatt and Friedman were both Orthodox Jews from New York who had received strong Jewish Zionist education and had spent substantial periods of time in Israel. Consequently, they seemed to understand the realities on the ground, certainly better than most Americans, so Trump apparently trusted that if he was elected, they would be able to fill in many of the important details that he wasn't so familiar with.

As for their opinions, it was clear that Friedman was strongly supportive of the settlement enterprise in Judea and Samaria, given his past substantial support to the communities of Beit El and Har Bracha in Samaria, just north of Jerusalem, including a building in Beit El that had been dedicated by him and his wife in honor of their parents. As a major donor to the community, Friedman once served as the president of the American Friends of Beit El Yeshiva, the US fundraising arm of its Jewish seminary and affiliated institutions, including high schools, an Israeli military prep academy, a newspaper with a religious Zionist orientation, as well as the conservative news site Arutz Sheva.

In 2003, a fellow by the name Donald Trump donated $10,000 to the organization in Friedman's honor, according to tax records for the Trump Foundation. Meanwhile, The Charles and Seryl Kushner Family Foundation, the philanthropic organization of Trump's son-in-law Jared

Kushner's family, donated $10,000 in 2011 and 2013, tax records show.

The Beit El Yeshiva is headed by Rabbi Zalman Melamed, while his son Rabbi Eliezer Melamed, is the rabbi of the Har Bracha community. Both rabbis strongly favor Israeli sovereignty in Judea and Samaria and have opposed a Palestinian state in the Land of Israel, views which Friedman has seemed, at least in past statements, to agree with.[36]

Jason Greenblatt is also connected to the settlement movement, though much less tightly and to a different branch of it. In the 1980s, he attended Har Etzion Yeshiva, a religious seminary in the Gush Etzion settlement of Alon Shvut in Judea.

Among yeshivas in Judea and Samaria, Har Etzion is considered to be among the more moderate and even left-leaning politically. It was founded by the late Yehuda Amital, a rabbi who ultimately came to support territorial compromise and a two-state solution. Amital was one of the founders of Meimad, a pro-land for peace religious party that eventually merged with the left-wing Labor Party.[37] Not everyone in that institution shared Rabbi Amital's political views, but his views did influence the overall political philosophy of the yeshiva on the question of land for peace. Then again, much has changed since then, including the years of terrorism that may have colored the views of many former students, including perhaps Jason Greenblatt.

Perhaps because of their slightly different perspectives, as well as their understanding of the realities on the ground, Greenblatt and Friedman were to serve the future president well, and to eventually play important roles in the new Trump administration.

On Election Day night 2016, defying the predictions of almost everyone in the mainstream media, even many of his supporters, Donald J. Trump won 306 to Hillary Clinton's

232 electoral votes, thereby becoming the 45th President of the United States.[38] The reaction to the Trump victory was not long in coming, and included public statements by Israeli politicians. Israeli Prime Minister Netanyahu hailed Trump's win, saying in a statement:

"President-elect Trump is a true friend of the State of Israel. We will work together to advance the security, stability and peace in our region. The strong connection between the United States and Israel is based on shared values, shared interests and a shared destiny. I'm certain that President-elect Trump and I will continue to strengthen the unique alliance between Israel and the United States, and bring it to new heights." [39]

Naftali Bennett, Education Minister and leader of the Jewish Home party, said in a statement after Trump's win:

"The era of a Palestinian state is over ... Trump's victory is an opportunity for Israel to immediately retract the notion of a Palestinian state in the center of the country, which would hurt our security and just cause." [40]

As could be expected, a sharply different perspective came from the Palestinians:

"We are ready to deal with the elected president on the basis of a two-state solution and to establish a Palestinian state on the 1967 borders." [41]
(Nabil Abu Rudeina, spokesman for Palestinian Authority President Mahmoud Abbas)

There was also a statement for "the Big Satan" from not-so-friendly Iran:

"Every US president has to understand the realities of today's

world. The most important thing is that the future US president sticks to agreements, to engagements undertaken." [42]

(Iranian Foreign Minister Mohammad Javad Zarif)

All in all, the stage was set for what was sure to be an exciting and eventful four to eight years with a new American leadership.

Chapter Four
American Jews – Who Are They?

"One day before I die, I will finally understand why liberals, especially Jewish liberals, fail to fully support Israel in its right to survive terror attacks." [1]

(Mike Gallagher, American radio host and political commentator)

Yes, this seems to be a question that talk show hosts, but not only talk show hosts, are very curious about. Some years ago, I was a guest on the Dennis Miller radio show and the host asked me such a question that was not easy to answer at the time, "What is the thing about Manhattan New York Jews and the Diaspora? I don't get it. Why are they so liberal?" [2] I must admit that I fairly adroitly avoided giving a direct answer, because, the necessary answer seemed so complex at the time. Yet, while the background is very complicated, there are some simple answers.

Miller was probably the first to ask me that question publicly, but during the next few years after that interview, I was asked variations of that question quite a few times, and I realized that this was a serious question that needed to be responded to. To do so, I had to confront some painful issues, but also to study the history of Jews in America.

While it's true that George Washington's Jewish friend, Hayim Solomon, was one of the unheralded founders of the United States, and while it's true that as early as the late eighteenth century, there were several important Sephardic Jewish communities that were quite traditional in their religious practice, as well as German-Jewish communities, mostly in the Midwest, the American Jewish population was literally transformed by the subsequent massive immigration from Eastern European countries. As opposed to the Sephardim, who traced their roots to the 1492 expulsion from Spain, most of the new arrivals were Ashkenazim, Jews descending years before from Germany/France, eventually immigrating to the countries of Eastern Europe.

In 1880, in a Jewish population of approximately 250,000, only one out of six American Jews was of East European extraction. Forty years later, in a community which had reached four million, five out of six American Jews had come from Eastern Europe. The newcomers tended to cluster in the poorer districts of the metropolises. Most of them settled in the great commercial, industrial, and cultural centers of the northeast (New York in the first place, then Philadelphia, Boston, and Baltimore) and of the Midwest (particularly Chicago). Certain neighborhoods in these cities became almost exclusively Jewish, congested and bustling with a rich, typically Jewish way of life. [3]

Through hard work and under extremely difficult conditions, these Jews established themselves in the garment industry, petty trade, cigar manufacture, construction, and food production. About thirty years after the beginning of the mass immigration, and not without bitter struggles, the Jewish trade union movement emerged as a formidable force, supported by over a quarter of a million workers. A flourishing Yiddish culture – poetry, prose, and drama – revolved mostly around the themes of the hardships of the Jewish worker's life, expressing the reality of daily existence within a community of immigrants. [4]

Economic pressures, opportunities for social promotion, the cult of liberty and individualism – all these contributed to the disintegration of Orthodox Jewry. How, for example, could one join the American race for success while observing the Sabbath? (Shabbat or Shabbos) [5]

My great-aunt, Becky Modlin, told the story of her early

immigrant confrontation with this culture shock:

In 1922, Becky left from Riga, Latvia to America (by boat) on the "S.S. Lithuania." She lived with her sister and her brother-in-law Rosie and Nathan Genkin (my grandparents), and for her, the adjustment was not easy.

"When I walked into their house one day, it was Yom Tov, Simchas Torah (a festive Jewish holiday celebrating the completion of the yearly Torah reading). I asked Rosie where Nathan was and she told me that he was working. I couldn't believe it. I felt like taking the boat and going straight back to Druya (the little town in present-day Belarus that she had lived in). In the place where I came from, even if you were very poor, on Yom Tov no one worked. We would go to shul and visit relatives and there would be a little something on the table. When she told me that Nathan works on Yom Tov, I felt so disappointed. Then a few days later on Saturday, the uncles came to see me. They all cried when I told them about my mother's passing. Later that day, Rosie said to me, 'Becky, put out the tea kettle.' So I put out the tea kettle, but I didn't make the fire. On Shabbos, I'll make the fire? That to me is like to kill somebody! She said to me, 'The tea's ready?' I said, 'It's ready, but it isn't boiling. I didn't make the fire.' She said, 'You'll have to learn.' When Rosie was in Druya, she would never light a fire on Saturday or work on a holiday, but I think Nathan changed her a lot. Nathan never went to shul and he wasn't religious. He didn't believe in it." [6]

In Eastern Europe, the phenomenon of Jews who weren't connected to their heritage was relatively new, having been influenced recently by the Haskalah, the movement of higher secular learning, that had been imported from Germany and had spread through portions of Russia, but in America, it seemed to be a given that to "make it", you had to abandon the "old ways". One of the new ways was Reform Judaism, imported from Jewish life in Germany by a previous wave of immigrants who had established Reform communities mostly in the Midwest and South.[7]

Reform Judaism grew greatly in the United States in the middle twentieth century, with Reform and an offshoot known as Conservative Judaism becoming the largest two religious movements in American Jewish life. The Reform movement originally evolved as a reaction to what was seen as the strictness of Orthodoxy, and its perceived incompatibility with success in German society. A similar process took place in America, to the extent that second generation Americans were looking for a form of Judaism that wouldn't make any 'primitive" ritual demands on them that might interfere with their newfound American lifestyle. American Jews, despite their unique heritage, totally threw themselves into American life and culture, much of which was actually Christian.

When the Reform movement started in Germany, the reformers abandoned the Shabbat as the distinctively Jewish day of worship. They abandoned the *kipah*, or yarmulke, the uniquely Jewish cap on the head, which recognizes that God is above us. They even had an organ in their synagogues to resemble the religious practice in the Catholic churches of Germany and other countries. The speed with which they ran away from traditional Jewish ritual was even shocking to some of their fellow reformers, who rebelled from the rebellion by restoring some of the Orthodox practice and creating a break-off faction. The hardcore ideological reformists ridiculed them and called them "conservatives", or those who are reluctant to change. The name stuck and in their new formation in America they established themselves as the Conservative Movement. For some time, it was a convenient middle ground, between Orthodoxy, with its firm adherence to tradition, and Reform, with its minimal rules, although as time passed, the Reform and Conservative moved closer and closer together in ritual observance, but also politically. For example, on June 2012, the American branch of Conservative Judaism formally approved same-sex marriage ceremonies in a 13-0 vote,[8] thereby moving themselves even closer to the Reform, who have, for a long time, been in the forefront of left-wing political action, including recently spearheading anti-Trump activism and protesting against his plans to increase border security against illegal immigration.[9] Therefore, it's important to remember that "Conservative Jews" doesn't mean "conservative Jews", as many of their views tend to be, on average, far more liberal than the mainstream of political conservatives.

Larry Feinstein, a social psychologist and self-described secular, Zionist Jew, shared his experience growing up in the Conservative movement in California:

"Jewish rituals and a connection to Israel were encouraged primarily as a way to maintain Jewish identity. Community leaders often asked, 'How Jewish are you?' Their attempt to balance tradition with modernity resulted in an ongoing struggle to maintain an identity, but without the intrinsic value of Jewish thought, ritual, or Israel." [10]

The abandonment of Jewish tradition in many families included the abandonment of the Sabbath, which had historically been an idyllic "island in time" for the average Jewish family, a full day of rest and family engagement from Friday evening to Saturday night. The busy work week is essentially set aside for an entire day. There are no computers, no televisions, and no cell phones; an island in time when all attention is focused on the family and the teachings of the Torah and its relevant commentaries that confront the important moral questions in our lives. It's a day when people actually talk to each other in a relaxed, direct way, without sending text messages!

"I was Jewish, through and through, although in our house that didn't mean a whole lot. We never went to synagogue. I never had a Bar Mitzvah. We didn't keep kosher or observe the Sabbath. In fact, I'm not so sure I would have known what the Sabbath looked like if it passed me on the street, so how could I observe it?" [11]

(Gilbert Gottfried, American-Jewish comedian)

The decreasing connection to Israel's biblical/cultural heritage and religious observance had ramifications for the continuity of American Jewish life. The first-generation Americans were still somewhat connected, and the love of learning, creative energy, and initiative that has always typified the Jewish community helped first and second-generation Jews to thrive in America, while remaining Jewishly connected to varying degrees.

"The real reason Jews don't have more Hanukkah music is that, historically, American Jewish singer-songwriters were too busy making Christmas music. 'White Christmas,' 'Rudolph the Red-

Knowing Who You Are: An Israeli teen reads from the holy scriptures (Torah) at the Western Wall during the celebration of his Bar Mitzvah.

Nosed Reindeer,' 'Silver Bells' and 'The Christmas Song (Chestnuts Roasting)' were all written by Jews." [12]

(Matisyahu, American Jewish musician/singer)

The problem was that with each generation, the connection to Jewish roots has been weakened even further to the point where the American Jewish community is intermarrying in droves, generally with secular non-Jews, thereby leaving their remnant of Judaism behind. Even more disturbing, large numbers aren't getting married at all. A study published by the Jerusalem-based Jewish People Policy Institute, found that only 50% of American Jews aged 25-54 (not including the ultra-Orthodox, or Haredi Jews) are currently married. Among those that are married, close to 60% married non-Jews. [13]

Within this group of non-Haredi Jewish-American adults, the study found the majority (60%) had no children living at home and that barely one-third (32%) were raising their children Jewish in some way or another.

These trends, the authors warn, combine to produce rather small numbers of Jews whose family circumstances are conducive to their own Jewish engagement and to the likelihood of their contributing to Jewish demographic continuity.

Only 15% of these American Jews, their analysis found, are married to other Jews and raising Jewish children at home. Another 8% are married to other Jews but have no children at home, 9% are raising their children as non-Jews, and 17% are married to non-Jews and have no children. The largest category – close to one-third – are unmarried Jews living on their own with no Jewish children at home. [14]

In short, the demographic prospects for the survival of the bulk of the Jewish community look bleak, and it appears to be gradually self-destructing. The current breakdown of the American Jewish community, by affiliation, is as follows:

According to a recent Pew Research Center study, approximately 10% of the 5.5 million American Jews consider themselves Orthodox in comparison to the 18% who consider themselves Conservative, 35% Reform, and 30% no denomination.[15]

If we want to understand the future of American Jewry and the social/political ramifications, it helps to examine the intermarriage rates, which vary considerably among the major US Jewish movements or denominations:

Virtually all Orthodox respondents who are married have a Jewish spouse (98%), and most married Conservative Jews also have Jewish spouses (73%). Half of Reform Jews who are married have a Jewish spouse. Among married Jews who have no denominational affiliation, 31% have a Jewish spouse.[16]

The stats are clear. The more observant the Jewish denomination, the more likely its members are to marry Jews, consequently strengthening their long-term Jewish commitment. Once again, we must emphasize that those figures don't include the majority of less-affiliated Jews that aren't even getting married, and therefore, the signs are not promising for that segment of the population.

Clearly, the exception to the self-destructive trends is the Orthodox community, in all of its different streams, loosely defined as those who believe that the Ten Commandments were given by God to Moses on Mount Sinai and who adhere most fervently to Jewish tradition and faith. For them, Judaism means much more than bagels and lox and a good Jewish deli, even if they do enjoy those culinary delights, at least as much as their less religious brothers and sisters. The emphasis in the Orthodox community, generally speaking, is less focused on past persecution of Jews and more on the miracle of modern-day Israel, less on sticking to liberal dogma and more on enjoying their families and honoring the Sabbath day. Or, as explained by one Orthodox rabbi:

"We do not limit our Jewish identities to reciting Catskills jokes (though we know them all) nor to building Holocaust memorials. And we proudly pledge allegiance to the flag of the United States of America, sing the "Star Spangled Banner" robustly, and – for the comparatively fewer among us who still follow NFL football – despise those who kneel when the anthem of the finest country ever conceived by humans is being played or performed." [17]

This is the community of Jews that on average marries relatively young, has larger families, and lower divorce rates. Even if some do leave the Orthodox fold over time, the movement has had much greater success at passing on Jewish tradition and faith to the next generation in greater numbers. Among those who have had children, nearly half (48%) of Orthodox Jews have four or more offspring, while just 9% of other Jewish parents have families of that size.[18] The impact of that is enormous. Within two generations, according to sociologist Steven M. Cohen of Hebrew Union College, the Orthodox faction of the American Jewish population has more than quintupled; and more than a quarter of American Jews seventeen years of age or younger are Orthodox.[19]

Which leads us to the political issues and the question that I was asked by Dennis Miller about the liberalism of American Jews. Issues such as school choice, abortion, same sex marriage, religious liberty, illegal immigration, the Israeli-Palestinian conflict, and the war on Islamic terror – all are issues on which Democrats and Republicans strongly disagree, but they are also issues on which the various segments of the Jewish community disagree. Consequently, the voting patterns of the American Jews tend to reflect where they fall on the religious spectrum, with those who have a stronger commitment to Judaism more likely to vote for the GOP. A post-election 2016 survey found sharp differences among the various denominations:

Among Jews overall, according to the Pew study, 70% say they are Democrats or lean towards the Democratic Party, while only 22% are Republican or lean Republican. For Orthodox Jews, however, the balance is in the other direction: 57% are Republican or lean Republican, and 36% are Democrats or lean Democratic.[20]

In the 2016 election, 54% of Orthodox Jews say they voted for Trump, according a new survey by the American Jewish Committee (AJC). That was well above 24% of Conservative Jews, 10% of Reform Jews, 8% of Reconstructionist Jews (roughly similar to Reform) and 14% of respondents who identify themselves as "just Jewish."

Conversely, Hillary Clinton garnered only 13% of the Orthodox vote, 60% of the Conservative vote, 78% of the Reform vote and 89% of the Reconstructionist vote.[21]

It's interesting to note that if 54% of Orthodox Jews voted for Trump and 13% for Clinton, that seems to leave many who didn't even respond, perhaps for fear of admitting in passionately liberal Jewish strongholds that they voted for Trump. It should be pointed out that in New York City, where most elected officials are Democrats, registered Republicans are a rare commodity.

Walking With the Liberal Bible: Senate Minority leader Charles Schumer in Congress carrying the "liberal's bible", *The New York Times.*

Nonetheless, what is clear is that the overwhelming majority of Orthodox Jews voted for Trump. This pattern persists in most polling, despite the fact that Orthodox Jews tend to be heavily concentrated in

Democratic stronghold states, like New York and California. Furthermore, that pattern of support has continued well into Trump's first term. Just eight months after his first year in office, 71% of Orthodox Jews approved of the president's performance, while only 27% disapproved, and this was several months before the president's recognition of Jerusalem as the capital city of Israel! [22]

According to another recent poll, published in August 2018 by Ami Magazine, a whopping 91.6% of Orthodox Jews from the tri-state area of New York, New Jersey, and Connecticut approved of President Trump's performance. Only 8.4% said that they were unhappy with the president's performance.[23]

"The gap between self-identified Orthodox and non-Orthodox respondents in their responses to our questions is striking. For a number of years, we've been seeing Orthodox respondents lean more heavily Republican and conservative on a range of socio-political issues, while, in greater numbers than other sub-groups, showing very solid support for Israel and great pride in being Jewish." [24]

(AJC CEO, David Harris)

The ramifications for American politics should not be understated. Jews have been in the forefront of political activism for many years on behalf of liberal causes and in the leadership of the Democratic party. It's not an exaggeration to say that Liberalism has become the new religion for many of these Jews and anyone who defies the liberal dogma is attacked for daring to express "sacrilegious" sentiments that contradict that dogma. For example, daring to oppose abortion on demand, daring to oppose same-sex marriage, daring to support strict limits on US immigration from Muslim-dominant countries, or daring to oppose a Palestinian state have all become grounds for being labeled anti-women, homophobic, Islamophobic, or supportive of apartheid. That is likely to change as the numbers of the less Jewishly-affiliated continue to plummet and the American Orthodox Jewish numbers continue to grow.

Indeed, in a few significant ways, Orthodox Jews more closely resemble white evangelical Protestants than they resemble other US Jews. For example, similarly large majorities of Orthodox Jews (83%) and white evangelicals (86%) say that religion is very important in their lives, while only about one-fifth of other Jewish Americans (20%) say the same. Roughly three-quarters of both Orthodox Jews (74%) and white evangelicals (75%) report that they attend religious services at least once a month. And eight-in-ten or more Orthodox Jews (84%) and white evangelicals (82%) say that Israel was given to the Jewish people by God – more than twice the share of other American Jews (35%) who express this belief.[25]

Clearly there are theological differences between Christians and Orthodox Jews, but the connection to Israel and to God is an unspoken conservative (small c) bond between the two groups. This may influence political alliances going forward, as the Jewish community continues to evolve.

In addition to this growing alliance of values between Christian Zionists and the more traditional Jews, one can expect that the stereotypical Jewish support for left-wing causes will decrease over time. This will be a natural, inevitable process, as Jewish organizational funding priorities will change, as a result of the continuing demographic changes in the American Jewish community. So, too, the GOP will increasingly cater to traditional Jewish concerns as they see that the more traditional Jews are an important and influential constituency for them. Some of those changes have already happened in the selection of Trump's top advisors. Let's explore some of those choices in the next chapter, as President Donald J. Trump enters the White House.

Chapter Five
The New Jews And Trump

"I only work with the best." [1]

(Donald J. Trump)

When employees and employers, even coworkers, have a commitment to one another, everyone benefits. I have people who have been in business with me for decades. I reward their loyalty to the organization and to me. I know that they'll always be dedicated to what we're trying to accomplish. [2]

(Donald J. Trump)

The transition period, followed by the first days of the Trump administration, were possibly more eventful than the campaign, and were quite revealing about the different direction in which the new president wanted to take the country. Despite the fiercest efforts of his opponents on the Left, as well as some GOP establishment anti-Trumpers, to label the president a boor of low intelligence, this was a man who had built a massive business empire. That doesn't happen by chance. It does happen through strong leadership and knowledge of how to find and work with the right people. So, too, in his administration. He was determined to hire the best and the brightest, but also individuals who would be loyal to him and to his agenda.

The forming of the Trump team was intriguing, as well, for what it showed about his connections with particular American Jews who were to become key players in his Cabinet and among his significant advisors. Liberal Jews had played important foreign policy roles in previous administrations, the most recent being the Obama administration's Ambassador to Israel, Daniel Shapiro, who was sharply critical of Israel's settlement policy and strongly supported the Iran deal. One particular harsh criticism leveled publicly by Shapiro prompted a public response from Prime Minister Benjamin Netanyahu:

Shapiro: *"Too many attacks on Palestinians lack a vigorous investigation or response by Israeli authorities; too much vigilantism goes unchecked; and at times there seem to be two standards of adherence to the rule of law: one for Israelis and another for Palestinians," said at the INSS security conference in Tel Aviv.*[3]

Netanyahu: *"The words of the ambassador, on a day in which a murdered mother of six is buried and on a day in which a pregnant woman is stabbed – are unacceptable and incorrect," a statement from the Prime Minister's office read. "Israel enforces the law for Israelis and Palestinians. The Palestinian Authority is the one responsible for the diplomatic freeze, and continues to incite and refuse talks."*[4]

One of the most important appointments made by President Trump was the naming of David Friedman as US Ambassador to Israel. For Friedman, strengthening the US-Israel relationship was a no-brainer. His late father, Rabbi Morris Friedman of Temple Hillel in the New York City suburb of North Woodmere, also served as president of the multi-denominational New York Board of Rabbis. A strong Zionist, Rabbi Friedman was a rabbi of a Conservative synagogue who had strong relations in the growing Orthodox community, at a time when the two movements were closer ideologically and cooperated more on communal challenges. Rabbi Friedman, in what was then a controversial move, probably due to the liberal views of some of his congregants and neighbors, warmly welcomed President Ronald Reagan to his synagogue in 1984, a couple of weeks before Election Day, and then to his home for a Sabbath lunch. The rabbi's wife, Addi Friedman, served a festive Shabbat meal with stuffed chicken cutlets, apricot noodle pudding, and shredded salad. For desert, she served a chocolate date-nut cake and an apple crumb cake. President Reagan loved the chocolate cake! [5] This visit was the first time a United States president had been received by an American synagogue since George Washington visited Touro Synagogue in Newport, Rhode Island in 1791.[6]

Sitting at the table was the rabbi's son, David M. Friedman and his wife, Tammy. Some twenty years later, Friedman began to perform legal work for Trump the businessman and they developed a friendship. In February of 2005, Rabbi Friedman died. When a Jew passes on, his immediate family observes the *shiva*, the post-funeral period during which children sit for a week in mourning to honor the parent's memory. In those seven days, visitors come to comfort the mourners in their time of emotional need. During the Friedman *shiva*, there was a blizzard in New York. Despite the terrible storm, and in the midst of the storm, Donald Trump drove out to Long Island from Manhattan to make the customary condolence visit to David Friedman, which was a great effort and a genuinely warm gesture that did not go unnoticed by the mourner.[7]

Now serving the United States as Ambassador to Israel, there is no doubt that the closeness and accessibility that Friedman has to the president, in addition to their mutual respect and warmth, has increased his impact within the administration. Despite an understandable shift in his public profile since the appointment, Friedman's views have been remarkably consistent through the years. With a second apartment in Jerusalem and a deeply-held personal belief that Israel has the right to decide where to allow building in

Religious Jew, American Patriot: US Vice President Mike Pence administers the swearing-in ceremony for David Friedman as the US ambassador to Israel in March of 2017 in Washington, DC. At right is Friedman's wife Tammy Sand, and their grandchildren.

Judea and Samaria (the so-called West Bank) and Jerusalem, Friedman seems to have influenced a change in direction for US policy that has led to an easing of pressure on Israel to halt construction permits and, of course, as Trump's eyes and ears in Israel, led to the December 2017 announcement declaring US recognition of Jerusalem as Israel's capital. The Jerusalem declaration, as well as the shifting of the sands concerning settlement, has been a political earthquake, reversing long-standing presidential policy. Land for peace and the two-state solution had been the American mantra almost since Israel's recapture of these areas in the defensive Six Day War of 1967. Through the Ford, Carter, Reagan, Bush I, Clinton, Bush II, and Obama administrations, the rebuilt Israeli communities in Judea, Samaria, and eastern Jerusalem were usually declared an "obstacle to peace" and sometimes far worse:

> *State Department spokesman (under Obama) John Kirby reaffirmed the US commitment to a two-state solution and longstanding opposition to Israeli settlement construction in the West Bank – referring in unusually harsh language to the enterprise's "illegality" – five days after President-elect Donald Trump announced he would appoint an outspoken settlements supporter, David Friedman, to be the next US ambassador to Israel.*
>
> *Speaking with MSNBC's Andrea Mitchell on Tuesday afternoon, Kirby responded to Friedman's nomination by saying the Obama administration's stance opposing settlement expansion covers "generations of US policy on both sides of the aisle."* [8]

In addition to the appointment of Friedman, President Trump appointed another Orthodox Jew, his son-in-law, Jared Kushner, as a Senior Advisor and Chief Middle East Advisor. Married to Trump's daughter Ivanka, an Orthodox convert to Judaism who also works for her father in a senior capacity, the Kushners and their three young children have been a first in Washington, a young glamorous Jewish power couple that lives their own variation of Orthodox Judaism. What that means in the minimal sense is that they eat kosher food and they carefully protect the sanctity of their family life and the Sabbath day, when computers and cell phones are turned off from Friday evening until Saturday night and they reserve that island in time for their children, for each other, and perhaps for their guests. They also go to synagogue on Shabbat and worship God as Jews have done throughout

An Amazing Blueprint for Family Connectivity: Ivanka Trump beautifully explains how being Sabbath-observant has strengthened her family life. In this photo, Ivanka walks with husband Jared Kushner and their children Arabella Rose Kushner, Joseph Frederick Kushner, and Theodore James Kushner, as half-sister Tiffany Trump looks on.

their history. As Ivanka describes it:

> *"We observe the Sabbath ... From Friday to Saturday we don't do anything but hang out with one another. We don't make phone calls. We're pretty observant, more than some, less than others. It's been such a great life decision for me. I am very modern, but I'm also a very traditional person, and I think that's an interesting juxtaposition in how I was raised as well. I really find that with Judaism, it creates an amazing blueprint for family connectivity."* [9]

Jared Kushner has been at Trump's side during most foreign trips and, in particular, has spearheaded the Middle East visits, along with Middle East envoy Jason Greenblatt. Having worked with David Friedman during the election campaign as advisors and also as a Trump Organization

Spreading Positive Energy in the Middle East: President Trump's Special Representative for International Negotiations Jason Greenblatt enjoys a falafel during his trip to Israel in August 2017.

attorney, Greenblatt, when not in Washington DC or the Middle East, dwells in the heavily Orthodox Jewish township of Teaneck, New Jersey. Since his appointment as envoy, Greenblatt has been all over the map trying to infuse the Middle East with some positive realism. As with Friedman and probably Kushner, as well, he seems to understand that "land for peace" should be, at best, an option, but only if the two sides agree to it. Likewise, with "the two-state solution". More on those issues later.

Jewish advisors in the Trump administration weren't just in the foreign policy realm. There have been Jewish economic advisors and Cabinet members in past administrations and the Trump administration is certainly no exception. It's no secret that many Jews in the United States have been successful in the fields of business and finance. A study of the Pew Forum institute from 2008 found that on average, the Jews are the richest religious group in the US: 46% of (American) Jews earn more than $100,000 a year, compared to 19% among all Americans. Another Gallup poll conducted (that) year found that 70% of American Jews enjoy "a high standard of living" compared to 60% of the population and more than any other religious group.

More than 100 of the 400 billionaires on Forbes' list of the wealthiest people in America are Jews. Six of the 20 leading venture capital funds in the US belong to Jews, according to Forbes.

Jews are well represented in Wall Street, Silicon Valley, the US Congress and administration, Hollywood, TV networks and the American press – way beyond their percentage in the population.[10]

If a visitor would land on Earth from another planet, he would probably think that American Jews have always been wealthy. The reality, however, is much different. We have already examined the social and religious history of American Jews, but one must learn a bit of their economic history, from poverty to education and private initiative, to truly and honestly understand the relative financial success of most American Jews:

Only several thousand Jews lived in the US upon its establishment on July 4, 1776. Most of them, known previously by the pejorative term, Marranos, were the Jews of Spain and Portugal who were forced to convert to Catholicism or to leave their countries. Many pretended to convert and secretly observed Jewish ritual in hiding, while others were exiled or escaped from Spain in favor of colonies in North America.

In the mid-19th century, some 200,000 Jews immigrated to the US, mostly from Germany and central Europe. Most of them were Reform Jews, well-established, who saw themselves as Germans and Americans more than as Jews. They scattered across the continent and set up businesses, from small stores and factories to financial giants like Lehman Brothers and Goldman Sachs.

The great wave of immigration began in 1882. Czarist Russia, which was home to about half of the world's Jews, went through a failed industrial revolution and was on the verge of collapse, while the Jews living in small towns became impoverished and suffered from cruel pogroms.

Within forty-two years, some two million Jews immigrated to the US from Ukraine, western Russia, Poland, Lithuania, Belarus and Romania. They made up 25% of the Jewish population in those countries, about 15% of the world's Jews, and 10 times the number of Jews who immigrated to the Land of Israel during that period. The US became the world's biggest Jewish concentration. The mass immigration to Israel began in 1924, when the US enacted tough laws which halted the immigration.

The immigrants arrived in the US on crowded boats, and most of them were very poor. Dr. Robert Rockaway, who studied that period, wrote that 80% of US Jews were employed in manual work before World War I, most of them in textile factories.

Many workplaces were blocked to the Jews due to an anti-Semitic campaign led by industrialist Henry Ford. Most of them lived in crowded and filthy slums in New York, mostly in Brooklyn and the Lower East Side (of Manhattan).

Many films and books describe the world established in those neighborhoods: Vibrant, but tough and brutal. There was a lively culture of cabarets and small Yiddish theaters, alongside a Jewish mafia with famous crime bosses such as Meyer Lansky, Abner "Longie" Zwillman, and Louis "Lepke" Buchalter, who grew up in the filthy alleys.

Many of the Jews, who were socialists in Europe, became active in labor unions and in workers' strikes and protests. Many trade unions were established by Jews.

The Jewish immigrants, however, emerged from poverty and made faster progress than any other group of immigrants.

Anti-Semitism weakened after World War II and the restrictions on hiring Jews were reduced and later canceled as part of the 1964 Civil Rights Act.

As they became richer, Jews integrated into society. They moved from the slums to the suburbs, abandoned Yiddish and adopted the clothes, culture, slang and dating and shopping habits of the non-Jewish elite.

Alongside the Jews, millions of immigrants arrived in the US from Ireland, Italy, China and dozens of other countries. They too have settled down since then, but the Jews succeeded more than everyone. Why? All the experts we asked said the reason was Jewish education. Jewish American student organization Hillel found that 9 to 33% of students in leading universities in the US are Jewish.[11] This, despite the fact that the Jewish population in the United States rarely surpassed 3% of the overall population.

It should be pointed out that the Jewish emphasis on study came from the Jewish tradition of comprehensive Torah learning that has continued to this day, mostly among the Orthodox. The value of intense learning and achievement has been passed on from generation to generation and is deeply engrained in the Jewish culture. Therefore, it's important to understand that there was never affirmative action for Jews, nor was it ever desired. The message from parents to children was always, "Work hard and you will achieve!"

"The Jewish tradition always sanctified studying, and the Jews made an effort to study from the moment they arrived in America," says Danny Halperin, Israel's former economic attaché in Washington. "In addition, the Jews have a strong tradition of business entrepreneurship. They progressed because many areas were blocked to them. Many Irish were integrated into the police force, for example, and only few Jews. The Jews entered new fields in which there was need for people with initiative. They didn't integrate into traditional banking, so they established the investment banking." [12]

In other words, American Jews didn't succeed *despite the fact* that there was discrimination against them, but paradoxically, *because* there was discrimination against them. They knew that they needed to work hard and think creatively to get ahead, which only made them work harder. Complaining about discrimination and having "days of rage" was not the Jewish way. Overcoming obstacles through hard work and creativity was. In fact, the rise of the tiny, modern State of Israel as an economic and military power and a bastion of freedom in a vast sea of oppressive Islamic countries, is a result of that enterprising hard-working positive spirit.

"The Jews were the first people to undergo globalization," says Rebecca Caspi, senior vice president of the Jewish Federations of North America (JFNA). "They had a network of global connections way before other nations, and a strong and supportive community. The Jewish communal organization is considered a role model for all other ethnic groups. It helped the Jews everywhere and especially in the US, which was always more open than other countries and provided equal opportunities, while on the other hand – wasn't supportive of the individual."

"The mutual help allowed poor Jews to study. My family is an example of what happened to millions. My grandfather arrived in New York with two dollars in his pocket. He sold pencils, and then pants and then other things, and in the meantime studied English, German and Spanish and established ties. "He had five children, and the family had a small store in Brooklyn. They got help from the HIAS Jewish organization, which allowed them to study. They were so poor that they didn't have money for textbooks, so the siblings helped each other. My father was the youngest, and until he started university the four older siblings had already managed to settle down, so they all helped him complete his medical studies."

"The Jews had to excel in order to survive," says Avia Spivak, a professor of economics and former Bank of Israel deputy governor. "I once had a student of Russian descent, who told me that his parents said to him, 'You must be the best, because then you might get a small role.' That was the situation of the Jews abroad, and in America, too, until the 1960s. The most prestigious universities didn't take in Jewish students, so they studied in colleges and got the best grades. When the discrimination disappeared, the Jews reached the top. The discrimination lessened in most countries. I think Jews succeeded in America in particular because capitalism is good for the Jews. Jews have a tendency for entrepreneurship, they study more and have quick perception, know how to seize opportunities and have networking skills. A competitive environment gives Jews an advantage." [13]

Some of the key economic advisors in the Trump administration just happened to be Jewish – just happened to be, because being Jewish wasn't directly relevant to their jobs. Unlike the foreign policy advisors cited earlier, whose extensive practical knowledge of Israel and the Middle East, as well as their particular skills, including language skills, could be attributable, at least partially, to their Jewishness, the Jewishness of the economic advisors was totally irrelevant to their professional responsibilities.

Top advisors such as Treasury Secretary Steven Mnuchin and Chief Economic Advisor Gary Cohn have played pivotal roles in the administration, especially in crafting the tax reform and tax cut plan, which was approved by Congress at the end of 2017. Their vast accomplishments, both before and during the administration, were a product of their achievements in education (in the case of Cohn, despite the learning challenge of dyslexia) and hard work on the job. Sure, no direct connection to Judaism, but definitely a reflection of the Jewish cultural heritage of hard work and education that had enabled the poor immigrant Jews of the early twentieth century to rise from poverty to economic success in the land of the free.

Likewise, for Stephen Miller, another senior advisor,

Not All Immigrations Are Equal: Stephen Miller was Trump's point man in expressing the reasons for the proposed travel ban from terror-producing countries. For this he was viciously attacked, with most of the criticism coming from American Jewish liberals, who castigated Miller for not giving Muslim immigrants from Syria the same open door that was given to Miller's Jewish immigrant grandparents.

although with him, it's a bit more complicated because of the controversial immigration issue, which has caused his critics to throw his Jewish immigration heritage at him in an attempt to deflate his arguments. A media savvy millennial, Miller has been a valuable point man for President Trump on the hot issue of immigration reform, in which the administration has been attempting not just to end illegal immigration, but also to prioritize legal immigration to favor those who can help the country, consistent with its values of hard work and private initiative, as well as preferring those who know, or can easily learn the English language. The new bottom line, according to President Trump, seems to be "What are the chances that the new arrivals will become productive American citizens?"

Miller has received much criticism for being a powerful Trump spokesman on this issue, and some of the attacks have been quite personal. Journalist Jennifer Mendelsohn challenged Miller through a project that she calls "Resistance Genealogy". Using public records and genealogical websites like Ancestry.com, Mendelsohn revealed Miller's Jewish immigrant family roots, to expose the presumed hypocrisy in his position. Mendelsohn tracked down his great-grandmother's line item in the 1910 census. The entry noted that four years after arriving in the United States, she spoke only Yiddish, not English.[14]

Aside from revealing her gross bias by naming her project after the leftist anti-Trump "Resistance" movement, Mendelsohn exposes her own ignorance and/or insincerity by taking an isolated characteristic to prove a much bigger point, and failing at that. Other liberal Jewish critics, including some Reform rabbis, have done the same:

"If I had the chance, I'd ask him about his own family's history," says Rabbi Sarah Bassin, of Temple Emanuel in Beverly Hills and a board member of Newground: A Muslim-Jewish Partnership for Change, "hopefully to elicit some degree of empathy for families that are experiencing the plight that I'm assuming his family experienced a few generations back." [15]

The fact is, that Miller is talking about the full immigration picture about one hundred years after his great-grandparents arrived, a totally different context, with immigrants flooding in from very different cultures. The United States as a Judeo-Christian civilization has suffered in recent years from an Islamic immigration that does not fit in well with America, and is in many cases in sharp conflict with the Judeo-Christian heritage on which the United States is based, seeking to transform the country to its own Islamic ways, which condone polygamy, wife-beating, and other forms of oppression of women.

This has caused a reaction from many concerned Americans. In a December 10, 2009 CNN interview, the generally well-respected Reverend Franklin Graham reiterated past statements that he had made calling Islam "an evil and wicked religion ... True Islam cannot be practiced in this country," he told CNN's Campbell Brown. "You can't beat your wife. You cannot murder your children if you think they've committed adultery or something like that, which they do practice in these other (Islamic) countries." Perhaps the most immediate and razor-sharp response came from The Council on American-Islamic Relations (CAIR). As previously alluded to, CAIR is a Washington-based Islamic organization which presents itself as a moderate Islamic-American civil rights organization, but the reality is far less altruistic, to say the least. In a letter sent to Rev. Graham, CAIR National Executive Director Nihad Awad called for an urgent meeting at which Graham would be offered accurate and balanced information about Islam. Awad wrote:

"I believe your views on Islam are unworthy of a respected religious leader and are based on misinformation and misconceptions that could be cleared up in a face-to-face meeting with representatives of the American Muslim community ..." [16]

On the surface, this sounds like a reasonable appeal for tolerance and dialogue, in order to clear up what appeared, to some, to be Rev. Graham's misconceptions about American Islam. The letter from CAIR Director Awad to Graham was well-publicized, but, in contrast, much less reported was the following quote from Omar Ahmed, Chairman of the Board of CAIR:

Islam isn't in America to be equal to any other faith, but to become dominant. The Koran should be the highest authority in America, and Islam the only accepted religion on Earth. [17]

It seems that CAIR's Chairman of the Board inadvertently clarified the real agenda of the organization. Likewise, CAIR spokesman Ibrahim Hooper stated in a newspaper interview that he hopes to see an Islamic government over the US someday, brought about not by violence but through education. [18]

Jews Chanting Liberal Mantras and Calling it Judaism: Jews and Muslims march together for solidarity against President-elect Donald Trump in front of the White House in December 2016. The fear of Jihadist Islam has been given the misnomer, "Islamophobia", denoting an irrational anxiety. However, the term is clearly politically motivated, as there is much to realistically fear from an ideology that supports wife-beating, sexual abuse of children, and violence against those who don't share your beliefs.

Trump and his advisors have been blasted by the Left for speaking out in favor of the proposed ban on immigration from certain Muslim nations and for his tough stance on preventing terrorism by better controlling the flow of immigration. These policy positions have been based on a sharp increase in Muslim terror attacks on American soil, as the Muslim immigration has simultaneously increased in the past few decades. For this, Trump has been blasted as a bigot and an Islamophobe by the ostensible defenders of civil rights. This is what happens when one expresses genuine concerns about a very real threat from immigration from certain countries. Rather than address the reasonable arguments made by those who favor the ban, it's easier to call Trump names and to hurl epithets at his advisors.

The original executive order, which Miller was involved in crafting, temporarily banned citizens of seven predominantly Muslim countries and indefinitely banned Syrian refugees from entering the United States. It also instructed the US to prioritize Christian refugees from the Middle East over their Muslim counterparts and was widely criticized by lawmakers on both sides of the aisle as well as civil rights groups, such as the American Civil Liberties Union, which said that the order discriminated against Muslims.[19]

The critics who pointed out Miller's Jewish immigrant family history, thereby, in their eyes, proving his hypocrisy, were missing an important point. Jewish immigrants have never sought to supplant the laws and the dominant culture of the countries in which they have dwelled. There are those who rush to the defense of Islam by pointing out the issue of fairness or discrimination. How can we impinge on religious freedom in the mosques? How can we complain about the growth of the Muslim population? Christians, Jews, or people of any other religion would never accept such an infringement upon their rights, so how can it be done to the Muslims?

Perhaps those same fairness advocates would even recall the biblical chapter about the Egyptian enslavement of the Hebrews, pointing to what appear to be similar complaints made by the Egyptian ruler Pharaoh that the Hebrew population was growing too quickly. Their challenging question is obvious: Why are the growing Muslims in Europe or America any different than were the Hebrews in Egypt or the Jews in any other country? Don't the Muslims also have the right to peacefully have large families?

The difference is this: It is clear – even plainly stated in Judaism – that a Jew is obligated to honor and respect the laws of the country that he lives in, and not to attempt in any way to change it. This has always been the instruction given by rabbinical leaders through the difficult centuries of Jewish dispersion amongst the nations. Jews have continuously internalized this tradition, honoring and respecting the laws and the norms of whatever country they have lived in.[20] This is fundamentally different than the message that Muslims hear from their religious leaders.

Before the Hebrews in Egypt were enslaved some three thousand five hundred years ago, they were characteristically loyal citizens of Egypt. They rapidly abandoned their unique religious traditions in order to assimilate, with the intent to be better accepted into Egyptian society. The Hebrews had no interest in rebelling against the prevailing system in Egypt. The same was true regarding the Jews of Germany before World War II.

Years earlier, many of the Jews in Germany began calling themselves Germans of Mosaic Persuasion. The Reform Movement in Judaism that had started in Germany many years prior, was conducted in an effort to more closely resemble the customs of the German Christian society in which they lived. The Reformists started using organs in their Sabbath services, stopped wearing head-coverings in synagogue worship and in some cases, even changed their Sabbath observance day to Sunday. All of this was done in an effort to fit in and be accepted by their Christian fellow citizens. Their primary loyalty was clearly to Germany and to their own personal self-interest as they perceived it – specifically to work hard and succeed as accepted citizens in German society – but changing Germany or its system of government, laws, and values or culture was never even considered nor desired, not by individual Jews and not by the Jewish leadership.

The contrast between Jews in the Diaspora (scattered around the world) and the European and/or American

Muslims could not be greater, as the obvious Jewish desire to blend into American society has never been replicated by the Islamic-American communities. Their insularity on one hand, and aggressiveness on the other, are two reflections of the Islamic desire to change America.

The liberal critics, try as they may to criticize Miller by pointing out his Jewish immigrant family background, will simply prove their dishonesty or their ignorance of Judaism and Jewish history.

"The Hebrew is never a beggar; he has always kept the law – life by toil – often under severe and oppressive civil restrictions." [21]
(President Benjamin Harrison, State of the Union Address, 1891)

While those restrictions are mainly in the past, at least in America, the point is that even when Jews were severely discriminated against, they always lived as loyal citizens, never seeking to change the culture or the laws of the countries in which they dwelled. The American Jews have enjoyed freedoms that would have been unimaginable years ago, and they have flourished as hard-working, creative, and enterprising citizens. In America's current immigrant reality, to distinguish between immigration from different countries and cultures is certainly not bigoted.

Jewish liberal groups have been actively involved in the opposition to President Trump's most recent ban on travel from a number of predominately Muslim countries. These have included several Reform Jewish groups like the Union for Reform Judaism, and groups that ingenuously claim to be more mainstream, such as the Anti-Defamation League (ADL), which spearheaded an amicus brief urging the Supreme Court to block the executive order.[22]

However, in a sign of the rightward-shifting demographic/ political trends in American Jewry that we spoke about earlier, the Zionist Organization of America (ZOA) filed an amicus brief with the Supreme Court *in support* of the ban. Unlike the ADL and the Reform groups, the ZOA has generally been supportive of Trump's policies. In its brief, it stated that the action did not amount to a "Muslim ban", nor did it violate the Constitution.

ZOA cited terror attacks by immigrants in Boston, San Bernardino, Orlando and Manhattan, as well as Europe, in its defense of the executive order:

"The Proclamation's vital purpose exemplifies our most fundamental, overriding value of protecting American lives." [23]
(ZOA President Morton Klein, statement)

To criticize the Trump immigration policy, and to compare it to the legal immigration of the early 20th century, is a bitter insult to all of the hard-working, America-loving Jewish immigrants, and to the millions of hard-working immigrants from Italy, Ireland, China, Cuba, and many other countries, who arrived legally at Ellis Island and other ports of entry, with the fierce desire to be loyal Americans. President Trump, along with his advisors and his allies in Congress, are doing their best to adjust immigration policy to do what is responsible: to keep Americans safe, in relative harmony, and in loyal service of their country.

The intense legal debate reached its pinnacle on June 26, 2018, when the Supreme Court upheld President Trump's travel ban affecting several, mostly Muslim, countries, offering an endorsement of the president's executive authority on immigration in one of the hardest-fought battles of his presidency.

The 5-4 ruling marked the first major high court decision on a Trump administration policy. Chief Justice John Roberts, who authored the conservative majority opinion, wrote that the order was "squarely within the scope of Presidential authority" under federal law. "The sole prerequisite set forth in [federal law] is that the President find that the entry of the covered aliens would be detrimental to the interests of the United States. The President has undoubtedly fulfilled that requirement here," he wrote.[24]

The Supreme Court ruling was a clear refutation of the anarchists on the Left, who have been vigorously pushing for a dangerous open borders policy. It was also a well-earned triumph for President Trump, as well as a sweet vindication for his greatly maligned advisor, Stephen Miller, after the very harsh personal attacks that had unfairly used his legal, loyal Jewish immigrant heritage to attack him politically. Through Miller, the president's critics had attempted to slander him as a racist, by regurgitating the big lie, that illegal immigration from the most terror-ridden Muslim countries is equal to loyal, legal immigration by honest hard-working Jews.

Chapter Six
Far Left And Far Right: Two Poles Of Intolerance

"Extremism thrives amid ignorance and anger, intimidation and cowardice." [1]

(Hillary Clinton)

Q uite an accurate statement, yes, but she left out one important word, "intolerance". The United States is a country that has shown a remarkable ability to grow and learn from its mistakes, thus moving from the intolerance of slavery to freedom and full civil rights, from lack of equal gender rights to full rights for women. Tolerance is indeed the engine that is the antidote to extremism.

"You know, to just be grossly generalistic, you could put half of Trump's supporters into what I call the basket of deplorables. Right? The racist, sexist, homophobic, xenophobic, Islamophobic – you name it. And unfortunately, there are people like that." [2]

(Hillary Clinton)

Basket of deplorables? Slandering many millions of Americans is not exactly the epitome of tolerance. Placing harsh labels on the many millions of people who disagree with you isn't the antidote to extremism; it's one of its main causes. The polarization that we have witnessed during the Trump presidency wasn't born in a vacuum, but was merely a continuation of and a reaction to, the divisiveness of the Obama years, when, in the name of change and hope, liberal dogma became the new norm and anyone who went against that new religion was labeled a racist, an Islamophobe, a homophobe, or a sexist.

Are Farmers Deplorable? Many Trump supporters have resented the bigotry expressed against those with conservative values. This supporter posed while waiting in line to hear President Trump speak at a rally in Louisville, Kentucky.

The seemingly new approach of the Left to attack and defame anyone who dares to go against their sacred *libereligion* wasn't born in a vacuum, but was established many years ago by the leftist ideologue Saul Alinsky. Before he died in 1972, Alinsky, who called himself a "community organizer," advocated "agitation", disrupting meetings and personal relentless attacks on "enemies". He was indirectly a mentor of none other than the young Barack Obama, who taught Alinsky's radical political philosophy for the ACORN political action organization in Chicago. As explained by political analyst David Horowitz:

"Revolutionary warfare, which is not about compromise, must be conducted through deception. Thus, the rules for the organizers of revolutions, laid down by Alinsky, are rules for deception." [3]

Affirmative Discrimination Against Everyone Else? Demonstration against President-elect Trump in Los Angeles in November 2016.

Interestingly, the concept of deception in radical left philosophy and the Islamic concept of *taqiyya*, or deception to further the cause of Islam, both serve well their matching goals of destroying the American system and Judeo-Christian civilization. Despite their divergent concepts of radical Socialist vs. Islamic rule, they cynically cooperate in their dishonest means to bring American liberty and justice to its knees.

These two political movements have cooperated extensively in the protests of the Left in recent years, with the mother of those protests being Occupy Wall Street, which took over Zuccotti Park and eventually much of lower Manhattan in late 2011 for several months, ostensibly to protest social and economic inequality and lack of "real democracy" around the world. The primary stated goal of the Occupy Movement is to "advance social and economic justice and new forms of democracy". The movement has many different scopes; local groups often have different focuses, but among the movement's prime concerns are how large corporations (and the global financial system) control the world in a way that disproportionately benefits a minority, undermines democracy, and is unstable.[4]

The protests started peacefully, but soon turned raucous, with many incidents of violence, vandalism, and sexual abuse reported, as the protests often evolved into riots, while spreading to over 82 cities and even worldwide.[5]

While they weren't among the main organizers of the protests, Muslim activists soon came to voice their support and to exploit the protest as a platform for their own issues.

Muslims associated with the New York Chapter of the Council on American Islamic Relations and the local Islamic Leadership Council came to express their grievances and to speak of social justice.

"We as Muslim New Yorkers are here today because we are in solidarity and support of Occupy Wall Street."
(Linda Sarsour, director of the Arab-American Association)

Imam Aiyub Abdul Baki of the Islamic Leadership Council delivered a sermon on social justice based on the Last Sermon of the Prophet Muhammad. In a veiled reference to Wall Street bankers, the Imam mentioned the Prophet's commandment against usury. He also noted US constitutional protections of religious expression, alleging that Muslim-Americans do not fully enjoy that right.

"We are also suffering; suffering racism and discrimination. Islam-bashing is on the increase."[6]

As could be expected of one who practices deception, he ignored the many reasons why Islam was under suspicion in America, such as the 9-11 attacks and the sharp increase in recent years of Islamic extremism and terrorism on American soil, which has only increased since then, and the well-documented support of American Muslim organizations for the various Islamic terrorist organizations.[7]

Occupy Wall Street was often compared by the Left to the conservative Tea Party Movement, but such a comparison gave undeserved legitimacy to the left-wing movement. While the OWS protests were at their peak, one Tea-Partier took umbrage at the comparison, which he felt was totally unjustified:

"There are three key characteristics that separate OWS from the Tea Party: First, the Occupy protesters pride themselves on provocative resistance to law enforcement and in some cases violence. Second, they disrespect public and private property. Third, and most important, the Occupy movement lacks a coherent guiding philosophy.

The September 12, 2009 Tea Party demonstration in Washington, DC, is a perfect example of the way Tea Partiers do business. Organizers planned for 100,000 Tea Party activists to show up on the National Mall, but more than one million turned out. In spite of the huge group of people, there was never an "angry mob" mentality. Protestors said "excuse me" and "thank you." No one was arrested and no property was damaged. No one told us to, but we picked up every bit of trash, even if it was not ours. In only a month of much smaller Occupy-related protests, hundreds of people have been arrested from New York City to San Diego and abroad, and in some cases protesters have resorted to physical violence. The property damage has been significant...

But the biggest difference between the Tea Party and Occupy Wall Street is that the Tea Party is bound by a common set of values based on freedom, responsibility and property rights. While the Tea Party members hold a diverse set of views on many issues, they are united in a desire for less government, lower taxes and more freedom.

Conversely, the Occupy Wall Street protesters are unified only by their hatred of the wealthy...

Their answer is more government, but more government has been the problem all along. Our answer is less government and more freedom. But with individual freedom comes individual responsibility and respect for private property. These are the values that bind us as a community. That's why freedom works.[8]

Then there was the serious problem of the widespread expressions of anti-Semitism in the Occupy Movement, a phenomenon, which sadly typifies much of the Far Left today in groups like Antifa and Black Lives Matter. Some glaring examples from a report in Commentary Magazine:

Defenders and supporters of Occupy Wall Street have tried to downplay the extent of anti-Jewish and anti-Israel hostility, but it was more prevalent than their initial denials suggested or their belated statements of concern conceded.

To begin with, any conspiracy theory that connects a tiny portion (in this case, one percent) of the population with exploitative banking practices is susceptible to taking on anti-Semitic undertones. This is especially the case when the list of supporters includes the American Nazi Party, Iran's Ayatollah Khomeini, Louis Farrakhan, white supremacist David Duke, Socialist Party USA, the Council on American-Islamic Relations, Hezbollah, 911Truth.org, International Bolshevik Tendency, and myriad other dubious organizations and individuals. With such comrades in arms, leaders of Occupy Wall Street ought to have been much on guard against anti-Semitic talk.

Nor was the hostility a matter of undertones only. The tone, very early on, was set in part by signs and messages that were overtly anti-Semitic. "Google: (1) Wall St. Jews, (2) Jewish Billionaires, (3) Jews & FedRsrvBank," read one sign. Another: "Nazi Bankers Wall Street." The man holding up a sign that read "Hitler's Bankers," upon being pressed by passersby to explain himself, replied "Jews control Wall Street." He was then asked whether the Fox News Channel had asked him to hold up the sign, presumably to make Occupy Wall Street look bad, and he responded, "F– Fox News. That's bulls-t. F-ing Jew made that up." Another protester, upon being interrogated by a skeptical elderly passerby sporting a yarmulke, brushed him away saying, "You're a bum, Jew."

Occupy Wall Street's group page on Facebook was littered with images of the title page of Henry Ford's notorious pamphlet, "The International Jew", as well as a picture featuring the phrase *Arbeit Macht Frei*, lifted from the entrance gate at Auschwitz (Nazi death camp), with the accompaniment: "We don't work for bad money." [9]

On a random visit to Zuccotti Park in October, three signs were observed ... that related to American foreign policy, two of which pertained specifically to Israel. One read: "Obama stop giving bunker buster bombs to an extremist Israeli regime. Stop being Israel's hit-man. AIPAC will still dump you in 2012." The second: "USA and Israel are criminal psychopathic nations, an axis of evil, mass murderers, financial predators if not stopped no one has a future! Hands off Iran." A small table exhibiting books for purchase was dominated almost exclusively by Marxist and Communist literature. Among the offerings, the one seeming anomaly was a book on Boycott Divestment Sanctions (BDS), an organization that seeks to isolate Israel on all fronts.[10]

As we've discussed, the Occupy Wall Street movement was the precursor of Antifa, Black Lives Matter, and other extreme-Left organizations that were prominent in the numerous anti-Trump demonstrations that were organized following the 2016 Trump victory.

Hundreds of demonstrators protesting Trump's swearing-in, many dressed in black, engaged in violent skirmishes with police near the White House, of a magnitude rarely seen at the time of a presidential inauguration. At least 217 people were arrested in the rioting, police said.

In the violence, knots of activists in black clothes and masks threw rocks and bottles at officers wearing riot gear, who responded with volleys of tear gas and stun grenades as a helicopter hovered low overhead.

At one flash point, a protester hurled an object through the passenger window of a police van, which sped away in reverse as demonstrators cheered. Earlier, activists used chunks of pavement and baseball bats to shatter the windows of a Bank of America branch and a McDonald's outlet, all symbols of American capitalism.

Multiple vehicles were set on fire, including a black limousine. A knot of people dragged garbage cans into a street a few blocks from the White House and set them ablaze, later throwing a red cap bearing Trump's "Make America Great Again" campaign slogan into the flames.[11]

Then came the massive Women's March, hailed by much of the mainstream media as peaceful protest, which to a great extent it was, but below the surface there was a sinister message, orchestrated by less than stellar individuals.

One of the four main organizers of the event was Linda Sarsour, a hijab-wearing American Muslim and the former head of the Arab-American Association of New York, who had been recognized as a "champion of change" by the Obama White House. It turns out that this "homegirl in a hijab," as one of many articles about her put it, has a history of disturbing views, as advertised by ... Linda Sarsour.[12]

There are comments on her Twitter feed of the anti-Zionist sort: "Nothing is creepier than Zionism," she wrote in 2012. And, oddly, given her status as a major feminist organizer, there are more than a few that seem to make common cause with anti-feminists, like this from 2015: "You'll know when you're living under Shariah law if suddenly all your loans and credit cards become interest-free. Sound nice, doesn't it?"[13] She has dismissed the anti-Islamist feminist Ayaan Hirsi Ali in the most crude and cruel terms, insisting she is "not a real woman" and confessing that she wishes she could take away Ms. Ali's vagina – this about a woman who suffered genital mutilation as a girl in Somalia.[14]

Ms. Sarsour and her defenders have dismissed all of this as a smear campaign coordinated by the Far Right and motivated by Islamophobia...[15]

In a strange selection of heroes, the official Twitter feed of the Women's March offered warm wishes to Assata Shakur. "Happy birthday to the revolutionary #AssataShakur!" read the tweet, which featured a "#SignOfResistance, in Assata's honor" – a pink and purple Pop Art-style portrait of Ms. Shakur, better known as Joanne Chesimard, a convicted killer who is on the FBI's list of most wanted terrorists.[16]

Like many others, CNN's Jake Tapper noticed the outrageous tweet. "Shakur is a cop-killer fugitive in Cuba," he tweeted, going on to mention Ms. Sarsour's troubling past statements. "Any progressives out there condemning this?" he asked.[17]

One of the other three organizers of the Women's March was Tamika Mallory, a young black activist who was crowned the "Sojourner Truth of our time" by Jet magazine and "a leader of tomorrow" by Valerie Jarrett, (formerly Senior Advisor to President Obama) ... Ms. Mallory, in addition to applauding Assata Shakur as a feminist emblem, also admires Fidel Castro, who sheltered Ms. Shakur in Cuba. She put up a flurry of posts when Mr. Castro died last year. "R.I.P. Comandante! Your legacy lives on!" she wrote in one. She does not have similar respect for American police officers. "When you throw a brick in a pile of hogs, the one that hollers is the one you hit," she posted on Nov. 20 (2017). Ms. (Carmen) Perez (the third of the four Women's March organizers) also expressed her admiration for a Black Panther convicted of trying to kill six police officers: "Love learning from and sharing space with Baba Sekou Odinga."

But the public figure these Women's March leaders (Sarsour, Mallory, and Perez) regularly fawn over is Louis Farrakhan. On May 11, Ms. Mallory posted a photo with her arm around Mr. Farrakhan, the 84-year-old Nation of Islam leader notorious for his anti-Semitic comments, on Twitter and Instagram. "Thank God this man is still alive and doing well," she wrote.[18]

Mallory added, in a targeted attack on President Trump and even more so, on Prime Minister Netanyahu, "Be clear: Donald Trump's wall + #muslimban + #deportation plan are all lines out of the #Netanyahu book of oppression"…

Mallory was citing the following quote from a conversation between Trump and Mexican President Enrique Peña Nieto:

"You know, you look at Israel – Israel has a wall and everyone said do not build a wall, walls do not work – 99.9% of people trying to come across that wall cannot get across and more," Trump told Peña Nieto, according to a report. "Bibi Netanyahu told me the wall works." [19]

Almost everyone in Israel, across the political spectrum, has supported the southern border wall that has halted illegal immigration to Israel. That Mallory views it as oppression exposes her dogmatic leftist biases, as opposed to Trump, who is at his core a pragmatist. From his perspective, unlike Mallory, it's not about ideology – If the wall works and stops illegal immigration, build it!

The third of the four organizers, Carmen Perez, a Mexican-American and a veteran political organizer, was named one of Fortune's Top 50 World Leaders. In the

Exploiting the Left to Promote Jihad and Hatred of Jews: Women's March organizer, Linda Sarsour, has hijacked left-wing activism to bash the Jews, the Zionists, and women who have courageously liberated themselves from the shackles of Islam.

fall, she posted a photo in which she holds hands with Mr. Farrakhan, writing, "There are many times when I sit with elders or inspirational individuals where I think, 'I just wish I could package this and share this moment with others.'" She's also promoted a video of Mr. Farrakhan "dropping knowledge" and another in which he says he is "speaking truth to power." What is Mr. Farrakhan's truth? Readers born after 1980 will probably have little idea, since he has largely remained out of the headlines since the Million Man March he organized in 1995. But his views ... remain as appalling as ever. "And don't you forget, when it's God who puts you in the ovens, it's forever!" he warned Jews in a speech at a Nation of Islam gathering in Madison Square Garden in 1985. Five years later, he remained unreformed: "The Jews, a small handful, control the movement of this great nation, like a radar controls the movement of a great ship in the waters." Or this metaphor, directed at Jews: "You have wrapped your tentacles around the US government, and you are deceiving and sending this nation to hell." He called Hitler "a very great man" on national television. Judaism, he insists, is a "gutter religion." [20]

It's not an exaggeration to say that those three organizers of the acclaimed Women's March on Washington, DC are the heart and soul of the Left's anti-Trump movement. Liberal Democrats, including one notable Jewish liberal who one may assume didn't do his homework beforehand, praised the organizers. That misguided individual was Senate Minority leader Charles Schumer, who called the protest "part of the grand American tradition." Meanwhile, the House Democratic leader, Nancy Pelosi, offered her congratulations to the march's "courageous organizers" and Senator Kirsten Gillibrand gushed about them in Time, where they were among the top 100 most influential people of 2017. [21]

Even so, the Dems haven't learned their lesson. Women's March 2018 went on as scheduled, with the very same organizers, despite the anti-Semitism and deception of Linda Sarsour and the others. Senate Minority Leader Schumer was this time remarkably silent, even though he was directly attacked by Sarsour for holding discussions with the White House about immigration:

"I'm talking to Chuck Schumer," said Sarsour, during a Washington, DC rally, in late February 2018. "I'm tired of white men negotiating on the backs of people of color and communities like ours. We are not bargaining chips."[22] Sarsour, as already noted, is a staunch Muslim whose complexion and features are very white, but she was obviously making a very disingenuous appeal to her Black Lives Matter/ Muslim home base. She knew that she could easily do so by attacking this particular famous white Jew, with absolutely no fear of response. Sadly, Senate Minority Leader Schumer is an anti-Trump leftist who willingly panders to anti-Semites like Sarsour, as long as they lead massive demonstrations against Trump. It would apparently go against his primary interest to respond appropriately to Sarsour's thinly veiled racism and anti-Semitism.

All of the events that we've discussed so far are the necessary background context needed to understand what happened in Charlottesville, Virginia, in August of 2017. The August 11-12 "Unite the Right" rally was organized to

Who is the Extremist? Right and left-wing demonstrators square off in violent skirmishes at the "Unite the Right" rally in Charlottesville, Virginia. Dozens were injured.

protest the removal of the statue honoring the Confederate general Robert E. Lee in Emancipation Park, which had been renamed by the city council from Lee Park in June 2016.

The rally occurred amidst the backdrop of controversy generated by what many saw as the politically-based removals of Confederate monuments in the South, but also the removal or attempted removals of other historical monuments in other parts the country. These have even included attacks on long-standing monuments honoring former presidents George Washington and Thomas Jefferson, ostensibly because they once owned slaves.

The Charlottesville event quickly turned violent after protesters clashed with counter-protesters, leaving more than 30 people injured. On the morning of August 12, Virginia governor Terry McAuliffe declared a state of emergency, stating that public safety could not be safeguarded without additional powers. Within an hour, the Virginia State Police declared the assembly to be unlawful. At around 1:45 p.m., a man linked to white-supremacist groups rammed his car into a crowd of counter-protesters about 0.5 miles (0.8 km) away from the rally site, killing one person and injuring 19. The alleged perpetrator, James Alex Fields Jr., was arrested and charged with second-degree murder.

The rally was believed to include the largest group of white nationalists to come together in a decade and the scene was, indeed, chaotic. Police dressed in riot gear ordered people out and helicopters circled overhead. The white supremacists and neo-Nazis were a loud and very noticeable part of the larger group that had gathered to protest plans to remove the statue. [23]

President Trump responded to the reports from Charlottesville with the following statement:

"We condemn in the strongest possible terms this egregious display of hatred, bigotry and violence on many sides." [24]

The president's statement was met with a chorus of criticism, mostly from the left side of the spectrum, but not only, for the fact that he didn't specifically mention white supremacists. He was also called out for his words "on many sides". Two days later, the president followed up on his previous statement, more specific this time around:

"Racism is evil. And those who cause violence in its name are criminals and thugs, including KKK, neo-Nazis, White Supremacists, and other hate groups are repugnant to everything we hold dear as Americans. Those who spread violence in the name of bigotry strike at the very core of America." [25]

Hard to disagree with what the president said, but because he hadn't spoken so clearly and specifically the first time, the Democrats and many in the media weren't willing to give him a pass. Even some in the GOP and in his administration, were unhappy about it. Chief Economic Advisor Gary Cohn, who is Jewish, was apparently very upset. Mike Allen and Jonathan Swan of the news website Axios reported ... Cohn was "somewhere between appalled and furious." [26] Some rumors had it that Cohn had considered resigning, but in a public statement, he made it clear that he had decided on a more constructive approach, doing the opposite of what the neo-Nazis would have wanted:

"I believe this administration can and must do better in consistently and unequivocally condemning these groups and do everything we can to heal the deep divisions that exist in our communities. As a Jewish American, I will not allow neo-Nazis ranting 'Jews will not replace us' to cause this Jew to leave his job." [27]

The pressure on Cohn to resign was indeed intense from the liberal establishment. As a Jew, there is perhaps nothing worse than being told that you are defending anti-Semites, but he made the wise decision by standing his ground. Not only did Cohn not leave his pivotal job in the Trump administration, but he was perhaps the most influential figure in the administration's success in passing its landmark tax reform plan in December of 2017. He has since moved on, but not before making his positive impact on the American economy. That would not have happened had he caved in to the media pressure to resign during the Charlottesville fiasco.

But what about the "many sides" question? Were there actually "violent sides", or just the neo-Nazis and white supremacists? Apparently, the Far Left was out in force, as well, and was involved in increasing much of the violent conflict. Radical Left groups like Antifa and Black Lives Matter were there, happily stoking the violence that the neo-Nazis had ignited. Yes, the Far Right started the trouble, even though many of the marchers were unfairly labeled as neo-Nazis since there were some who were just concerned about the removal of historic statues, which in some ways does remind us of book-burning and the shutting down of opinions that you don't agree with. Nonetheless, the provocative neo-Nazi signs and chants expressing bigotry, racism, and anti-Semitism were what the media focused on, and understandably so. At the same time, it was clear that the Antifa and Black Lives Matter leftist movements, whose own anti-Semitic credentials were quite strong, were there with their very own helmets and clubs, clearly seeking a fight with the marchers. So, while not all marchers on the Right were violent anti-Semites or racists, and not all of the protesters on the Left were either, the result was that the extreme violent anti-Semites were fighting the extreme violent anti-Semites.

For those who say that those on the Left can't be anti-Semitic or racist, Black Lives Matter (BLM), for example, has been guided to anti-Semitism by the concept of "intersectionality", which argues that all oppressions are interlinked and cannot be solved alone. Somehow from this they conclude, with not a shred of evidence, and it's in the BLM platform, that Israel is carrying out "genocide" against the so-called Palestinians. BLM activists have visited Gaza and expressed a sympathetic attitude towards terrorist groups like Hamas, which does call for the genocide of Jews and actively engages in some of the most brutal forms of terrorism, including bus bombing, shootings, stabbings, and rock-throwing ambushes.[28]

A couple of years ago, a group of BLM activists from Chicago, visiting Israel on a fact-finding tour, were brought to Shiloh. Their stated purpose was to see the projects of the

Shiloh Israel Children's Fund, which I had founded some years ago after my then three-year-old son and I were shot and wounded in a terror attack. We visited our main therapeutic-educational campus, where so many Israeli children, victims of Islamic terrorism, have been treated for trauma.

Despite receiving what is for most visitors a moving, informative learning experience about the challenges faced by the residents of the biblical heartland communities (otherwise known as "settlers"), they spent much of their time complaining about the "crimes" and the "genocide" that they claimed Israel is guilty of. Their ignorance was appalling and one of the gentle, sensitive therapists who heard everything was in shock and couldn't understand where the blind hatred was coming from.

Back to Charlottesville, where the march turned into a violent brawl, in which the most extreme on both sides turned their hatred against each other and thus, against everyone around them. In a law-abiding country, protests should be peaceful and flames are to be extinguished, not stoked. Even some of the left-leaning media noticed what was really happening. Sheryl Gay Stolberg at *The New York Times* tweeted the following:

"A few rapid thoughts from Charlottesville. Number one, striking how many of the white nationalists were young people, almost entirely men." Her second tweet: "The hard Left seemed as hate-filled as the Alt-Right. I saw club wielding Antifa beating white nationalists being led out of the park."

And then this in the *Washington Post* by David Weigel:

(Headline) Fear of 'Violent Left' Preceded Events in Charlottesville.
"On Saturday afternoon, shortly before her camera captured

a car plowing through left-wing activists in Charlottesville, killing one and injuring more than a dozen others, Faith Goldy (Canadian writer and commentator who provided live coverage of the events) warned that the Left was spinning out of control." [29]

The clashes at the rally were indeed harsh. The neo-Nazi thugs will most likely continue their agitations when permitted, as will their opponents on the Far Left. In truth, the differences in principle between them aren't that great. Both sides are intolerant of those who disagree with them and both sides don't hesitate to resort to street violence against those with whom they disagree. But that is not the American way, nor is it consistent with free speech.

In one of the more unusual cases of teenage peer pressure leading to disaster, sixteen-year-old John Daly was forcibly recruited into a white supremacist Skinhead organization in central Florida and was nearly murdered by the same group when they learned of his Jewishness. Lured to a beach at night by the group leader, Daly was badly beaten and left for dead. His "comrades" punched him, kicked him, and held his head under water until he lay lifeless, but he survived. That was almost thirty years ago. Shortly after his attackers were released from jail, Daly moved to Israel and has become an authority on the white supremacist movement and extremist movements, in general.[30] What was his view of Charlottesville?

"Having attended Klan rallies as an attendee and as a demonstrator, I can tell you that the Far Right arrives expecting to be hated, whereas those on the Far Left that come ready to fight (helmets, shields, clubs, etc.) don't come to demonstrate but to instigate. 'If one of us gets hurt it works to the benefit of all due to the media coverage it will bring ultimately showing the righteousness of our cause,' is the unspoken operating agenda of many of the members in

A True Freedom Fighter: Civil Rights leader Dr. Martin Luther King Jr. not only spoke out and sacrificed on behalf of freedom, but courageously criticized the hatred and the incitement to violence of the Black Muslims.

attendance. I've seen it with my own eyes and watched it on TV. The Charlottesville event was a gathering of a number of different disenfranchised individuals wanting to seem like they belonged to something larger. When you start pulling people like that together you will – invariably – also draw many extremists willing, and more importantly, wanting to draw attention to the 'righteousness' of their cause through violence. To the extreme Right, reckless violence is just another language of the world and the extreme Left has learned to speak the same 'language' in return." [31]

After the chaos in Charlottesville, one may have hoped that cooler heads would have prevailed in Congress. Since that day, most level-headed politicians have, and the president certainly has, quite publicly called repeatedly for calm, for love, and for unity. Unfortunately, not everyone on the Left is listening.

Rep. Keith Ellison, D-Minn., the deputy chair of the Democratic National Committee, caused a stir on social media in early 2018, when he posed with a book promoting the violent "Antifa" movement. In a January 2018 post on Twitter, Ellison said that he found the book "Antifa: The Anti-Fascist Handbook" at a Minneapolis book shop and gleefully proclaimed that it would "strike fear in the heart of @realDonaldTrump." [32]

Interesting, violent words coming from someone who is now a mainstream leader in the national Democratic Party. Then again, perhaps we shouldn't be surprised, given Ellison's close ties to racist anti-Semite Louis Farrakhan, leader of the White-hating, Jew-hating, America-hating Nation of Islam. Perhaps we shouldn't be surprised, given his ties to the Hamas terrorist organization, and to the radical Muslim Brotherhood. Nor should we be surprised, given his $50,000 in campaign contributions that were given or raised by officials of the Council on American-Islamic Relations (CAIR), which was spun off of the Hamas front group Islamic Association for Palestine (IAP). And yes, perhaps we shouldn't be surprised, given his Jew-baiting political campaigns.[33]

The other force is one of bitterness and hatred, and it comes perilously close to advocating violence. It is expressed in the various black nationalist groups that are springing up across the nation, the largest and best-known being Elijah Muhammad's Muslim movement.

(Martin Luther King Jr., Birmingham, Alabama, April 16, 1963)

However, the real problem is that it isn't just Ellison who cavorts with anti-Semites. What about the other Democrats in Congress – California Rep. Maxine Waters, New York Rep. Gregory Meeks, California Rep. Barbara Lee, Texas Rep. Al Green, Louisiana Rep. William Jefferson, Illinois Rep. Danny Davis, and Indiana Rep. Andre Carson – all of whom are known to have attended meetings with Farrakhan or attended Nation of Islam conventions, with several even attending a recent dinner that included Iranian President Hassan Rouhani? [34]

But the anti-Semitic and anti-Israel trends in the new Democratic Party go way beyond the Congressional Black Caucus and its members who we have cited above. In a Democratic primary shortly before the 2018 midterm elections, Alexandria Ocasio-Cortez, a 28-year-old Democratic Socialist, handily defeated ten-term Congressman Joe Crowley (D-NY), who had been widely expected to eventually succeed Nancy Pelosi as leader of the Democrats in the House of Representatives. Ocasio-Cortez is openly and proudly affiliated with the Democratic Socialists of America, which supports the boycott, divestment, and sanctions (BDS) movement targeting Israel. She pointedly referred to Israel's defense of its Gaza border against mobs of Hamas terrorists as "a massacre", after many of the terrorists were killed while attempting to breach the border, launching firebombs and rocks attacks at Israeli soldiers.

"The Left is on the move, and mainstream Democrats, in order to be successful, must stop the denial," veteran New York political consultant Hank Sheinkopf reported. "Traditional urban organizations are the emperors with no clothes. This trend expedites the long-running divorce proceedings between the Democratic Party and Israel." [35]

The winds of hatred and violence on the Far Left are reaching new and frightening levels, as even some politicians are legitimizing the thuggery by calling for violence against those with whom they simply disagree. In fact, Congresswoman Maxine Waters (D-CA), mentioned previously, has very publicly and unabashedly adopted the violent tactics of Antifa, actually encouraging violent harassment and attacks against Trump administration Cabinet members, advisors, and their supporters. Vowing to bring the "resistance" to a new level, she urged supporters to swarm Cabinet members at gas stations and anywhere else they're seen.

"If you see anybody from that Cabinet in a restaurant, in a department store, at a gasoline station, you get out and you create a crowd and you push back on them and you tell them they're not welcome anymore, anywhere," Waters said. Making it clear that this is part of an organized strategy, she later told MSNBC that protesters are "going to absolutely harass them." [36]

The results of such Antifa-inspired violence has been the violent harassment, in separate June 2018 incidents, of White House Press Spokeswoman Sarah Huckabee Sanders, Senior Advisor Stephen Miller, and Homeland Security Secretary Kirstjen Nielsen. In one particularly egregious attack, Florida Attorney General – and ardent Trump supporter – Pam Bondi was confronted by a group of protesters outside the screening of a documentary about Mister Rogers in Tampa. Whitney Ray, a spokeswoman for Bondi, told the Tampa Bay Times that a video of the incident shared on social media showed only a small portion of what actually happened.

"The video they are choosing to share is of the least aggressive portion of the attack that transpired after police arrived to control the scene. What they are not sharing publicly are several previous encounters involving large men getting in the Attorney General's face, spitting and blocking her exit," Ray said.

Fox News reported that Bondi, who, ironically, was watching a documentary about the avuncular children's entertainer Mr. Rogers, didn't exactly think that the activists' behavior aligned with what Mr. Rogers had taught.

"We were in a movie about anti-bullying and practicing peace and love and tolerance and accepting of people for their differences," she said. "We all believe in free speech, but there's a big difference there." [37]

The rapidly increasing intolerance on the Left and the intentional use of violent tactics, even advocated by a Congresswoman in the party of Truman and JFK, is a frightening trend that we should all be concerned about. To their credit, Senate Minority Leader Charles Schumer and

House Minority Leader Nancy Pelosi criticized Rep. Waters' not-so-veiled call to violence, although Pelosi's statement prefaced her critique with a direct swipe at President Trump. Sadly, far too many prominent Democrats, as well as most of the Trump-bashing mainstream media remained silent, or similarly qualified their mild criticism of the harassment strategy by first blaming Trump for what Pelosi referred to as his "daily lack of civility that has provoked responses that are predictable but unacceptable."

Unfortunately, I can't say I'm surprised by this growing trend in America of adopting Antifa's strategy of violent intolerance, but that trend, formerly the province of the neo-Nazis on the extreme Right, is rapidly becoming a central strategy on the American Left, as evidenced when a conservative speaker or an Israeli is invited to speak on a college campus and is heckled or violently attacked by leftist thugs. For the Left, the new "justice" seems to be shouting down and threatening those who disagree with you. What is truly scary is that the establishment Left in politics and in the mainstream media is starting to legitimize it. Shouldn't we all be just a little bit disturbed that this may be the future of the Democratic Party?

Chapter Seven
The Land Of Israel And Peace

"I often hear them accuse Israel of Judaizing Jerusalem. That's like accusing America of Americanizing Washington, or the British of Anglicizing London. You know why we're called 'Jews'? Because we come from Judea." [1]

(Benjamin Netanyahu)

"You can always count on Americans to do the right thing – after they've tried everything else." [2]

(Winston Churchill)

Every new president is asked about his peace plan for Israel and its neighbors. President Trump was no exception.

Successive American administrations have tried to bring peace to Israel and its neighbors, but, to their great frustration, these efforts have failed miserably, at the cost of billions of dollars, thousands of hours of effort, and thousands of Israelis killed or wounded by the resultant terror attacks. Despite the best of intentions, it hasn't worked. How can we understand such a colossal failure, and, perhaps more importantly, how can we comprehend the inability of president after president to get the message that it's time to try a different approach?

Since Israel was reestablished as an independent, sovereign nation in 1948, the land of Israel has been bombarded with a nearly ceaseless torrent of wars and terrorism to a disproportionate degree never before experienced in human civilization. Surrounded by enemy nations, assaulted by terrorist organizations from the north, from the south, and from within, Israel's political leadership nonetheless has always been obsessed with the search for peace. It didn't matter that the Arab nations surrounding Israel were perpetually threatening to "drive the Jews into the sea" both before and after each war, in which those stubborn Jews always somehow emerged victorious. Even so, Israel's political leadership has always expressed its willingness to withdraw from conquered lands in exchange for genuine promises of peace or, until recently, the absence of war. In modern history, it is almost unheard of for the winning nation to surrender land that it has rightfully taken possession of in a defensive war. Indeed, it is rare for the victor to do anything other than to dictate the terms of the truce and/or peaceful resolution to the conflict.[3]

Nonetheless, what has come to be known as the "Peace Process" has always been based on the "Land for Peace" formula, which has always meant that Israel, a tiny country about the size of New Jersey, is expected to divide up its country, to hand over its historical heartland for the promise of peace.

If Israel as a whole were to reject out of hand this strange and skewed system of international abuse, it would certainly be reasonable and it would garner no little amount of respect, if not love, but sadly, that is not the case. Israel has legitimized the demands by agreeing in principle to negotiate the surrender of at least some of Israel's heartland communities and even part of its capital city, as if it's an intricate jigsaw puzzle game in which each piece has no intrinsic value. It has accepted as a basic premise that tiny Israel, and only tiny Israel, is the one that needs to surrender land as part of any potential peace agreement. Furthermore, Israel has implicitly agreed to accept random terrorist attacks, often with little or no response beyond verbal protest. This has created dangerous precedence and greatly decreased Israel's power of deterrence. Under this strangely unbalanced system of international relations in the rules of war and diplomacy, the many Arab nations, with their huge land mass over 700 times the land mass of Israel, those same nations who badly lost their war of aggression in 1967, are under no obligation to surrender even an inch of the lands that they control. However, little Israel, the country that won those territories fair and square in a defensive war, is expected to return what it recaptured in the war. We can complain about the inherent lack of fairness in this arrangement that is imposed on us by outside parties, but we can't expect to alter the lack of fairness if the political leadership of Israel has accepted its legitimacy.

As Israel's first prime minister, David Ben-Gurion would often say:

"It doesn't matter what the goyim (non-Jews) say. What matters is what the Jews do." [4]

The term "Goyim" literally means nations, but in general use refers to nations other than Israel. Did Ben-Gurion's statement mean that the newly reestablished State of Israel would ignore the appeals and the concerns of friendly nations like the United States? Certainly not, but it does mean that when Israel is faced with existential decisions or any other decisions of Zionist principle, meaning issues relating to our national sovereignty, any Israeli leader that succumbs to foreign commands is severely lacking a sense of national responsibility. Therefore, in 1948, after a successful battle against Arab invading armies, Ben-Gurion was pressured to retreat. Despite the relative weakness of Israel at that time, he refused the diplomatic onslaught. Likewise, when Prime Minister Golda Meir was pressured by US President Richard Nixon to retreat to the 1949 armistice line and redivide Jerusalem, she responded proactively by not only refusing Nixon's demands, but by building new Jewish neighborhoods in formerly Jordanian-occupied parts of the city. Prime Minister Levi Eshkol followed the same principle, building the Jerusalem neighborhood that came to be called Ramat Eshkol, despite pressure to halt Jewish building in the areas of the capital that had been liberated in 1967.

In other words, we can't expect the non-Jewish world to change the unfair status quo, if we ourselves don't have the fortitude to fight against an unfair and unjust treatment that ties our hands and prevents us from asserting our national destiny. As opposed to Ben-Gurion's proclamation of Jewish independence, current Prime Minister Netanyahu has always been a strong proponent of not taking steps to assert Israeli sovereignty, without at least tacit approval from the White House.

Even during the difficult Obama years, when Israel was lectured and scolded often by Obama, Hillary Clinton, and John Kerry, for even allowing one Jewish family in the central mountainous region of Judea or Samaria (the so-called West Bank) to expand a home, Netanyahu still tried to get American approval for Israeli building policy in those areas. That, notwithstanding the fact that Israel recaptured these areas in a defensive war, the Six Day War of 1967, and that is precisely where Israel has repeatedly been told that it needed to allow an independent state for the Palestinians. For that reason, Netanyahu has always been reluctant to act in favor of a more proactive Israeli development policy.

President Trump came into the White House, as previous presidents had, suddenly confronted with the Israel-Palestinian conflict and being asked what he will do to make peace. Unlike his predecessors, however, Trump approached the issue with the pragmatism of the smart businessman that he was. Trump the real estate developer would carefully examine every potential investment, studying its history to see where there had been successes and failures in the past, in order to determine its prospects for the future. Trump decided to learn the issue of Middle East peace before committing to the land for peace formula, the two-state solution, the peace for peace formula, or any other formula in the Middle East. He wasn't prepared to immediately start spouting any slogans about Israelis or Palestinians until he fully understood the issues in all of their complexities. And yes, there was certainly a lot to learn.

Have you ever wondered how this whole dispute began? In the year 63 CE (Current Era), the Roman rulers exiled the Jews from the Land of Israel, where they had thrived as a sovereign nation for well over a thousand years. At that time, the land, no longer the unified Kingdom of Israel that had existed in the era of Kings David and Solomon, had been divided into two parts. The northern region was known as Israel, while the southern region was known as Judea. The Romans did away with both of those names and renamed the entire country "Palestina", a Roman derivative of the term "Philistines", which referred to the nation that was an arch-enemy of Israel, the folks that brought us the infamous Goliath who had fought against the future king who was then just little David. The Romans understood the power of semantics and sought to linguistically erase the biblical, historical names of Israel in one fell swoop. What better way could there be to wipe a country off the map than to change the name of its homeland, where its citizens had dwelled as a sovereign people for over a thousand years and in a semi-sovereign status for several hundred more?

In truth, the Roman strategy worked, but only to a limited extent. For nearly two thousand years, the people of Israel were scattered around the world, persecuted, forced to abandon their faith, expelled from countries, harassed, and even murdered by the millions. The few who remained in what came to be known as Palestine to almost everyone, lived in poverty in a barren, decrepit land in which hardly a tree grew, hardly a flower bloomed, and disease was rampant. [5]

This, from one famous person, who visited the Land of Israel about one hundred and fifty years ago:

"We traversed some miles of desolate country whose soil is rich enough but is given wholly to weeds – a silent, mournful expanse ... A desolation is here that not even imagination can grace with the pomp of life and action. We reached Tabor safely ... We never saw a human being on the whole route. We pressed on toward the goal of our crusade, renowned Jerusalem. The further we went the hotter the sun got and the more rocky and bare, repulsive and dreary the landscape became ... There was hardly a tree or a shrub anywhere. Even the olive and the cactus, those fast friends of a worthless soil, had almost deserted the country. No landscape exists that is more tiresome to the eye than that which bounds the approaches to Jerusalem ... Jerusalem is mournful, dreary and lifeless. I would not desire to live here. It is a hopeless, dreary, heartbroken land ..." [6]

(Author Mark Twain, on his visit to the Land of Israel)

Despite the lowly state of the Jewish people and the lowly state of their ancestral homeland, they continued to pray with faces pointed to the Land of Israel. Every day, devout Jews would cry out to their Creator at least three times a day for the return to the Land of Israel. Most people, even many Jews, didn't believe that the return to the Land was even a remote possibility. After all, what nation has ever been exiled from its land, bounced from country to country, suffered unparalleled horrors, yet despite everything, returned to reestablish itself again as a sovereign nation in its ancient homeland? Yet, as absurd as it seemed, for believing Jews, it was a given, the essence of being a Jew was to pray for the eventual and expected return.

"Blow the great shofar (ram's horn) for our liberation, and raise up a miracle to gather our exiles, and gather us together from the four corners of the earth; blessed are You, O Lord, who gathers the dispersed of His people Israel."
(From the Amidah prayer, recited by devout Jews three times daily)

"For I will take you from among the nations, and gather you out of all the lands, and will bring you into your own land."
(Ezekiel 36:24)

Sure enough, in the late 19th century, the people of Israel started to come back to their tiny piece of land at the crossroads of three great continents. It started out as very small groups of tens that eventually became hundreds and then thousands. Life was very difficult for them. At first there was no economy, little farming, and lots of serious diseases, including malaria. The challenge of returning to the homeland was overwhelming for some, but there was no turning back.

The process continued. In the Zionist movement, President Trump's famous expression "Drain the swamps" was meant to be understood literally! It didn't refer to Washington, DC political hacks, but to the actual swamps that were drained by the Jewish pioneers, who worked long hours to create agriculture to feed the people.

New cities were built. Old cities and towns were rebuilt. An economy was developed where there was none. Trees started to grow, the desert started to bloom, and the land began to give of its fruit once again.

And guess what else started to happen in the 1920s as this amazing process was well underway? Arab immigrants from the neighboring Arab-inhabited lands flocked to this new Jewish country in the making, looking for opportunities in a growing economy. Joining together with some of their Arab brethren who already lived there, they soon began to agitate against their Jewish neighbors, sounding the Arab war cry of *"Itbach al-Yahud!* – Kill the Jews".

In the 1920s, terrible pogroms (violent riots) were carried out by Arab mobs in the cities of Jerusalem, Tsfat (Safed), and Hebron. The scourge of rapes of Jewish women and the increasing fear of Arab snipers on the roads was ever-present and was interspersed with wild rampages of outright murder.[7]

Our review of these early conflicts in the land that was then known to the world as Palestine brings us back to our previous discussion about the so-called Palestinians. The Arab residents in the Land of Israel in the early part of this century didn't refer to themselves as Palestinians. In fact, if you called yourself a Palestinian, you were most likely one of the Jewish residents. Most of the Arabs seemed to follow the lead of their religious and political leader, the Grand Mufti of Jerusalem, Haj (Muhammad Effendi) Amin al-Husseini, the radical pro-Nazi Muslim leader, scion of the influential

Friend of the Nazis: Palestinian Arab leader Haj Amin al-Husseini meets with Nazi kingpin Adolf Hitler, urging him to establish concentration camps to imprison/kill Jews in the Land of Israel.

Husseini family of Jerusalem. Husseini was an ardent Arab nationalist. The thought of creating a separate Arab nation called Palestine was the farthest thing from his mind. No, he wanted to unite all of the Arabs as one nation and established the Arab Higher Committee, to work towards his stated goal of driving the "Zionists" out of the Land. Toward this end, he met with Adolf Hitler's second in command, Adolf Eichmann, in late 1937, when Eichmann visited Palestine to discuss the possibility of establishing concentration camps and deporting Jews to there. Husseini later met with Hitler, as well. His collaboration with the Nazis is well-documented.[8]

Husseini's grand plans of developing his own final solution didn't come to fruition. Even though six million Jews were slaughtered by the Nazis, Husseini's hope of driving out their brethren from the Middle East never materialized as Israel's gradual return soon turned into a return to Jewish sovereignty.

With the end of the League of Nations in 1945 after World War II, the British, who had been authorized to rule over Palestine since 1917, surrendered their mandate. The United Nations was established and the new body eventually gave its approval in 1948 for a truncated Jewish State of Israel, with its historic capital, Jerusalem, to be internationalized. Though its borders reflected only a small fraction of the historic Jewish homeland, it was a cause for celebration, as the sovereign nation of Israel officially returned to its Land after almost two thousand years of exile and national homelessness.

The Arabs rejected the UN vote and declared war on the nascent state. The State of Israel declared its independence on May 14, 1948 and the Arabs, surrounding Israel on all sides, and heavily outnumbering its meager army, both in weaponry and soldiers, launched a coordinated war against Israel. The war was extremely painful, both in terms of deaths and territory lost to Israel's people. Almost one percent of the population of the reestablished Jewish nation fell in the fighting, many of whom were civilians. The historic, biblical, mountainous regions of Samaria and Judea and eastern Jerusalem had fallen into the hands of the newly independent Kingdom of Jordan, which had been established just twenty years earlier on the eastern side of the Jordan River. The southern region of Gaza was taken by the Egyptians and the Golan Heights on the country's northern peaks by the newly independent Republic of Syria.[9]

At the end of the war, Israel was left an extremely narrow country with a dangerous east to west bottleneck just nine miles wide. This fragile, almost indefensible situation continued for nineteen years, with the threats from the east, north and south, both stated and implicit, growing greater every day.

"We intend to open a general assault against Israel. This will be total war. Our basic aim will be to destroy Israel." [10]
(Egyptian President Gamal Abdel Nasser, May 26, 1967)

"The sole method we shall apply against Israel is total war, which will result in the extermination of Zionist existence." [11]
(Egyptian Radio, Voice of the Arabs, May 18, 1967)

"I, as a military man, believe that the time has come to enter into a battle of annihilation." [12]
(Syrian Defense Minister Hafez al-Assad, May 20, 1967)

"The existence of Israel is an error which must be rectified ... Our goal is clear – to wipe Israel off the map." [13]
(Iraqi President Abdul Rahman Aref, May 31, 1967)

The result of these verbal attacks and the military maneuvers that accompanied them was the Six Day War in June of 1967. Once again attacked from all sides, Israel fought another valiant war of survival and the results

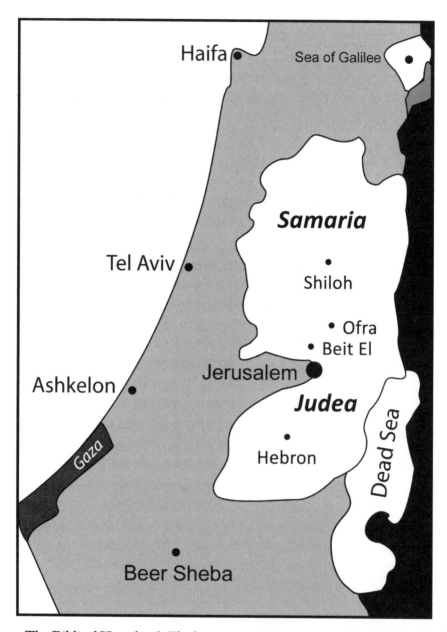

The Biblical Heartland: The historic, strategic regions of Samaria and Judea comprise the so-called West Bank, which much of the world wants Israel to surrender for the establishment of another Muslim terror-dominated Arab country.

were nothing short of miraculous. Israel recaptured the mountainous regions Judea and Samaria, with its biblical cities of Bethlehem, Shiloh, Jericho, Shechem, Beit El, and Hebron. These places were the cradle of Western civilization, the sites where most of the biblical stories took place, and with much archeology proving the factuality of those stories. Probably the greatest highlight of the war was the recapturing of eastern Jerusalem, including the Temple Mount (Mount Moriah) and its famous Western Wall, which had often been called the Wailing Wall, because of the tears that had been shed there through the years of dispersion by Jews who somehow managed to come to pray at the site, near the ruins of the Holy Temple. Their tears were joined in spirit with the tears that were shed by those Jews who couldn't get there physically but cried daily over Zion's destruction. As an outcome of the fighting, Israel also recaptured the strategic Golan Heights in the north, the vast Sinai desert in the south, and the Gaza Strip region on the southwestern coast.

The dangerous, fragile borders of Israel that had existed from 1948-1967 have been known to many as "The Auschwitz Borders", thus aptly titled as such by Israel's Foreign Minister Abba Eban, in bitter memory of the notorious Nazi death camp of the same name:

"We have openly said that the map will never again be the same as on June 4, 1967. For us, this is a matter of security and of principles. The June map is for us equivalent to insecurity and danger. I do not exaggerate when I say that it has for us something of a memory of Auschwitz. We shudder when we think of what would have awaited us in the circumstances of June 1967, if we had been defeated; with Syrians on the mountain and we in the valley, with the Jordanian army in sight of the sea, with the Egyptians who hold our throat in their hands in Gaza. This is a situation which will never be repeated in history." [14]

(Abba Eban, Israeli Foreign Minister)

Blowing the Shofar of Jerusalem's Liberation: IDF Chief Rabbi Shlomo Goren, carrying the Torah scroll, blows the Shofar (the ram's horn) celebrating Jerusalem's liberation in the Six Day War – June of 1967, at the Western Wall in Jerusalem.

The Six Day War was a great victory for Israel, but not just because of the geographic strategic depth that it provided. The miraculous nature of the triumph affirmed the uniqueness of Israel, for what other nation but the original biblical nation wins a war in six days and on the Sabbath day they rest? Furthermore, it was a rare, yet classic return to roots story, as the territories that Israel recovered from Jordanian occupation were the biblical heartland of Judea, Samaria, and Jerusalem, Israel's raison d'être, its most powerful claim to the Land of Israel. It's important to remember that King David's unified kingdom was based in ancient eastern Jerusalem, not in the relatively new coastal city of Tel Aviv. Samuel the Prophet grew up into prophecy in Shiloh in the heart of Samaria, not in the relatively new resort city of Netanya, while the Patriarchs and Matriarchs of Israel are buried in Hebron in Judea, not in the relatively new city of Petach Tikva. The region that the world likes to call the West Bank is in reality the biblical heartland of Israel and the cradle of Western, or Judeo-Christian civilization. Any Jew and any Christian who pressures Israel to surrender those areas is denying his or her roots and the biblically-based roots of Western Civilization.

On the other hand, if we are speaking about deep roots in the land, shouldn't we also address the origins and deep ties to the land of the Palestinians? After all, even if the Romans invented the name, aren't today's Palestinians a legitimate people with legitimate rights in what they call their ancient homeland?

Chapter Eight
Palestinians, Peace And Reality

For they have healed the hurt of the daughter of my
people slightly, saying, Peace, peace – when there is
no peace.

(Jeremiah 8:11)

The reality, that many of those who know prefer to
ignore, is that the Palestinian people were created
by the Arabs in 1964, or perhaps it became official
in 1974.

Just three years before the Six Day War, in May of
1964, the Arab League, which was comprised of fourteen
Arab countries, had established the Palestine Liberation
Organization (PLO), as a political/military body to deal
directly with the problem of the Palestinian Arabs. The PLO's
first leader was an Egyptian, Ahmed Shukairy. In 1969,
the most notable leader of the PLO – Fatah leader Yasser
Arafat – was elected chairman of the new organization with
its immediate goal being to create a Palestinian people and
use it as a tool to wipe "the Zionist entity" off the map. Up
until that point, the term Palestinian had referred more to
Jews than to Arabs or Muslims. My father-in-law was born
in Jerusalem in 1939, nine years before the State of Israel
was established, to parents with deep roots in the Land of
Israel, that can be traced back ten generations. To this day,
he continues to assert that, if there is such a thing, he is far
more of a Palestinian than Cairo-born Arafat ever was. He
repeatedly emphasizes that the only people who even used
the term Palestinians to describe themselves were Jews and
that most Arabs of the Land of Israel, who considered

Arab Leaders Meet in Cairo, 1970: (L-R) Libyan leader Muammar Khadafy, PLO chief Yasser Arafat, Egyptian President Gamal Abdel Nasser, and King Hussein of Jordan.

themselves part of "the Arab nation", refused to use the term Palestinians, until many years later, when it became politically expedient to do so.

Ten years after the PLO was founded, at the 1974 Rabat Summit of Arab nations, which included the PLO, it was decided to reaffirm the armed struggle against Israel, and a unanimous resolution was passed which, for the first time, declared the PLO to be the "sole legitimate representative of the Palestinian people."

It also declared that the Arab world would accept any parts of the Land of Israel that Israel would decide to surrender peacefully. Thus, began the policy of shooting at Israel and bombing Israel with one hand, while simultaneously having "peace" negotiations with the other.[1]

It's always necessary to know the history in order to understand the present beyond the surreal world of media spin. The Palestinians that everyone speaks of were officially born at the Rabat Summit of 1974. They are certainly not an indigenous people deprived of their rights. However, the politicians of the world seem to accept otherwise. The Palestinian narrative has been adopted and promoted wholeheartedly by the purveyors of political correctness, for whom Israel had long ago ceased to be a fashionable cause. In fact, it is nearly impossible for a public speaker to burst the bubble of an indigenous, long-suffering Palestinian people without being fiercely attacked by radical leftists from organizations like Antifa on college campuses. Their arrogance and intolerance towards those who can easily refute their arguments is only matched by their ignorance of the Middle Eastern facts on the ground.

The illusion of an indigenous, formerly sovereign Palestinian people is perhaps the greatest hoax of modern times, designed to deceive an uninformed public. Peace can only be achieved if we have a realistic understanding of who we are dealing with and what the facts are. There needs to be a clear definition of terms, starting with the term "peace."

"Peace for us means the destruction of Israel. We are preparing for an all-out war, a war which will last for generations." [2]
(PLO Chairman Yasser Arafat, Jordanian Television, September 1993)

Incredibly, those words were spoken on September 13, 1993, the very same day that the PLO and Israel signed the Oslo Accords in a lively celebration of the so-called peace process at the White House. And what a day it was! In an event that was designed to get the maximal media exposure, then PLO negotiator Mahmoud Abbas and Israeli Foreign Minister Shimon Peres signed the document for their respective sides at a ceremony on the White House lawn, witnessed by President Bill Clinton, Secretary of State Warren Christopher, Russian Foreign Minister Andrei

Kozyrev, Israel's Prime Minister Yitzhak Rabin and PLO Chairman Yasser Arafat.

Negotiated in secret between Israel and the PLO, the Oslo Accords envisaged a withdrawal of Israeli forces from parts of the Gaza Strip, as well as Judea and Samaria (the West Bank), and their replacement by a Palestinian National Authority (PA). The PA would be given limited rule, to be known as autonomy, over the major Palestinian population centers in the West Bank and Gaza for a five-year interim period, during which further transfers of land to the PA would be discussed. The idea of a phased transition to Palestinian rule was intended to build mutual trust for negotiating a final-status agreement – the most difficult issues, namely Jerusalem, refugees, Israeli settlements, security, water rights and borders were purposefully left to the end in the hope that a successful interim period would make people on both sides more amenable to compromise.[3]

The first phase, which mainly consisted of Israeli withdrawal and transfer of land, cities, and towns in Judea, Samaria, and Gaza to the PA, was implemented, but it was a source of great political turmoil in an Israel that was fearful of what the second phase would bring in its wake. Sure enough, the Oslo Two agreement of September 1995 advanced agreements on security issues, PA elections, further transfer of land, transfer of civil power from Israel to the PA, trade conditions and release of Palestinian prisoners who had been jailed for past terrorist attacks on Israeli civilians.

Israeli politicians like Shimon Peres and Yossi Beilin, the architects of the Oslo Accords, loudly proclaimed a "New Middle East", asserting that Israel needed to recognize that the "times-they-were-a-changing", with the title of the old Bob Dylan song suddenly seeming appropriate to a Middle Eastern context. However, Israel was deeply divided and apprehensive about the new situation, especially since there were so many doubts about the sincerity of their new-found peace partners.

"The Jihad (Islamic holy war against unbelievers) will continue, and Jerusalem is not (only) for the Palestinian people, it is for all the Muslim nation ... you have to come and to fight and to start the Jihad to liberate Jerusalem." [4]
(PLO Chairman Yasser Arafat, May 10, 1994, speaking in a mosque)

Shortly afterwards, when word had gotten out about his peace-shattering speech, Arafat was approached by throngs of Western reporters who confronted him about the obvious contradiction of being committed to resolving differences of opinion peacefully and publicly calling for Jihad, or holy war, to conquer Jerusalem for all of "the Muslim nation." He wrinkled his face with that sly smile that he was known for, and proclaimed, "I will continue my Jihad for peace!" It was an obvious oxymoron that none of the perplexed journalists seemed to know how to respond to, but who could blame them?

For the past twenty-five years, the Palestinian leadership has spoken about peace on one side of its mouth, while encouraging terror attacks through funding and incitement on the other side. This has been going on for at least two decades, but the approach has continued to be expanded in recent years, and the figure continues to rise. In 2016, the PA distributed $300 million to terrorist prisoners and their families, but the PA paid terrorists and their families over $347 million in 2017. Terrorists sentenced to three to five years in Israeli prisons receive the average income of a Palestinian, $580 per month, while those who committed more severe crimes and were likely involved in killing Israelis, receive five times that amount each month for the rest of their lives. This is according to the official PA budget online and it's all legal under the PA's morally convoluted system of laws under current PA Chairman Mahmoud Abbas. This amounts to an officially sanctioned, and internationally-supported, PA government incentive system to kill Israelis.[5]

As alluded to earlier, my three-year-old son and I were victims of one such Fatah (Palestinian Authority sponsored) terror attack at the end of 2001, when we were shot and wounded while driving home from Jerusalem. I was shot in the leg and my son was shot in the head by terrorists armed with AK-47 assault rifles. The bullet that crashed into my son's head and through his neck missed his brain stem by just one millimeter, and he survived. I was declared the 1,000th terror victim to be hospitalized in that hospital, just in that previous year and a half, which was the first part of the second intifada, the PA's terror war on Israel. Despite the frequency of the terror attacks, which were almost a daily occurrence at that time, if you asked some of the naive politicians, they would have told you that these are simply the challenges on the road to peace.

Since those exciting, pie-in-the-sky days of the Oslo Accords, when politicians on both sides of the ocean foolishly thought that peace was at hand, nearly 1,700 Israelis have been murdered in terror attacks, with thousands of other innocent civilians wounded during that same time period. [6]

These have been the years of the so-called peace process, an era of intermittent negotiations, during which former Israeli Prime Ministers Ehud Barak and Ehud Olmert each offered to surrender 90-100% of Judea and Samaria and most parts of eastern Jerusalem for a Palestinian state. This included some form of Palestinian control of the Temple Mount, the site of the ruins of the Holy Temple that had stood there at two intervals of several hundred years each, including during the reign of King Solomon. Barak's offer was rejected out of hand by Yasser Arafat in 1999, as was Olmert's similar offer rejected by Mahmoud Abbas in 2008. [7]

The Friendliness Before the Storm: President Trump and Leader of the Palestinian Authority Mahmoud Abbas, 2017, in the Oval Office of the White House.

During the Obama years, efforts were made to get Netanyahu to agree to a similar arrangement, and he did agree to the concept of a two-state solution, but it wasn't going to work for several reasons, each of which was a game-breaker:

1. Netanyahu's governing coalitions, unlike those of Barak and Olmert, were Center-Right, and therefore, less willing to agree to major land concessions in the historic biblical heartland of Israel.

2. After twenty-five years of Palestinian Authority lies and deception, Israelis were less trusting of any promises of peace that would be signed in exchange for the concrete security risks that further surrender of land would entail.

3. Abbas and his cohorts had upped the ante, demanding another freeze on all building in the Jewish communities

A Real Partnership: President Trump has restored genuine cooperation and discreet consultation to the US-Israel relationship.

of Judea, Samaria, and eastern Jerusalem. Without such a guaranteed freeze, he refused to negotiate. Meanwhile the terror attacks continued, with Abbas' obvious blessing.

Jumping ahead to the present, there is a new sheriff in town, and his name is Donald J. Trump. Unlike Obama, President Trump has repeatedly emphasized that while he would like to make what he has called "the ultimate deal", he is not going to attempt to force it through at the expense of the Israel-US relationship. Both on the Iran issue, on which he sees eye to eye with the Israeli consensus, and by declaring American recognition of Jerusalem as Israel's capital, Trump has already shown his friendship to Israel to an extent way beyond any other president in American history since Israel's reestablishment in 1948.

"We know what a person thinks not when he tells us what he thinks, but by his actions." [8]

(Jewish author Isaac Bashevis Singer)

Less than two years after his election in 2016, President Trump was already fulfilling his campaign promises as they pertained to Israel. Let's examine them one-by-one:

Trump Quote – Iran: "My number-one priority is to dismantle the disastrous deal with Iran ... We will totally dismantle Iran's global terror network." [9]

Reality: After giving Congress and the European Union ample time to substantially improve it, President Trump cancelled the Iran deal, creating new facts on the ground in an already tumultuous situation. While America's European allies certainly weren't happy at the rejection of their appeals to stay in the agreement, the president made it clear that the United States would not let itself be hoodwinked by the lying Ayatollahs in Teheran (more on that later). The Trump administration has wisely strengthened America's relationships with Saudi Arabia, Egypt, and other Sunni Muslim countries that are also very concerned about stopping Shiite Iran's race to nuclear capability. Furthermore, and partially due to Trump's leadership and encouragement, there is covert cooperation between Israel and the Saudis on this issue, which may be spreading to other issues. All secretly, of course, and all denied by the Saudis.

Trump Quote – The United Nations: "The UN is not a friend of democracy, it's not a friend to freedom, it's not a friend even to the United States ... and it surely is not a friend to Israel ... I will veto any attempt by the UN to impose its will on the Jewish state." [10]

Reality: After the bitter finale to the Obama administration, in which it allowed UN Resolution 2334 to pass in December 2016 with fourteen yes votes and an American abstention, and which stated that Israeli settlements have "no legal validity" and represent "a flagrant violation under international law", US Ambassador to the UN, Nikki Haley, has sharply turned the tide. Haley has been a strong voice at the UN, passionately defending the US recognition of Jerusalem as Israel's capital, proudly defending and explaining the reasons for Trump's slashing of funding for certain anti-Israel, American-funded agencies like UNWRA, which actually had knowingly provided cover for Hamas terrorists and their weaponry during the last Gaza war.

These bold moves culminated with the withdrawal from the United Nations Human Rights Council in June of 2018. Ambassador Haley called the 47-member council "a protector of human rights abusers, and a cesspool of political bias", while pointing out that in the first half of 2018, "the UNHRC passed five resolutions against Israel, more than against any other country ... If the Human Rights Council is going to attack countries that uphold human rights and attack those that abuse human rights, then the US should not provide it with credibility," she concluded.[11]

Trump Quote – US Embassy: "We will move the American embassy to the eternal capital of the Jewish people, Jerusalem." [12]

Reality: On December 6, 2017, President Trump formally announced the United States recognition of Jerusalem as the capital of Israel, reversing nearly seven decades of a discriminatory American foreign policy, and ordered the planned relocation of the United States embassy from Tel Aviv to Jerusalem. Vice President Mike Pence proudly

Palestinians in Bethlehem Declare, "Americans Go Home!": In the birthplace of Jesus and King David, Palestinians protest President Donald Trump's announcement to recognize Jerusalem as the capital of Israel in December of 2017. Holding portraits of Vice President Mike Pence and President Trump's Special Envoy, Jason Greenblatt, the demonstrators made it clear that Pence and Greenblatt were not welcome in Palestinian-controlled Bethlehem.

announced during his emotional January 2018 visit to Israel that the Embassy will be moved before the end of 2019. Subsequently, the State Department confirmed an expedited timing of a temporary move, with an official telling *The Times of Israel*: "We are planning to open the new US Embassy to Israel in Jerusalem in May (2018). The Embassy opening will coincide with Israel's 70th anniversary." The official said, "The Embassy will initially be located in Arnona (in south Jerusalem), on a compound that currently houses the consular operations of Consulate General Jerusalem. At least initially, it will consist of the Ambassador and a small team." In short, the promise of moving the US Embassy was kept,[13] and speedily, on May 14, 2018!

Trump Quote – The Peace Process: "Palestinians must come to the table willing to accept that Israel is a Jewish state and it will forever exist as a Jewish state." [14]

Reality: Palestinian Authority Chairman Mahmoud Abbas, in a speech given to the Palestine Liberation Organization's Central Council, shortly after the Jerusalem announcement, once again denied that there are any Jewish historical ties to Jerusalem. He then either cursed or threatened President Trump, saying, "May your house be destroyed!" One can only wonder which Trump house the Palestinian "Peace Partner" was referring to – The White House or Trump Tower in New York City?

The insults have only continued and intensified. In a speech in Ramallah in March of 2018, Palestinian Authority Chairman Mahmoud Abbas said:

"The United States legitimizes settlements. That's what American officials do, and at their head, in Tel Aviv, is (US Ambassador to Israel) David Friedman. He said, 'They're building on their own land.' The son of a dog, they're building on their own land? He himself is a settler, and his entire family are settlers." [15]

Ambassador Friedman, who lives in the Ambassador's residence in Herziliya, just north of Tel Aviv, and who previously lived in New York, immediately responded to Abbas' charges. Speaking at the Global Forum for Combating Anti-Semitism, Friedman said:

"Three Jews were killed in cold blood by the Palestinian terrorists, and the reaction from the Palestinian Authority was deafening. No condemnation whatsoever. I pointed that out, without further adjectives, without further commentary ... His response was to refer to me as the 'son of a dog.' Anti-Semitism, or political discourse? Not for me to judge. I'll leave that all up to you." [16]

Former Trump rival, Sen. Ted Cruz responded to the Palestinian Authority's (PA) name-calling on Twitter, tweeting, "The Palestinians continue to slander @ USAmbIsrael David Friedman, who instead deserves tremendous praise for honorably representing the US," and added in a follow-up tweet, "If the PA is looking for incitement and glorification of violence, they need only look in a mirror. They pay $400 million in monthly salaries/ benefits to terrorists & their families to incentivize/reward terrorism against Israel." [17]

The Jerusalem decision didn't occur in a vacuum, rather it was a case of Trump's resoluteness in standing against the firm opposition of the entrenched "Arabists" at the State Department, headed by Secretary of State Rex Tillerson. Unfortunately, Tillerson had been no better than Clinton or Kerry on foreign policy issues pertaining to Israel, including siding with the Palestine Liberation Organization and the Palestinian Authority against a group of American citizen terror victims who had filed a lawsuit against the terror organizations. In February of 2018, after an extended internal debate that included officials from the State Department and the Justice Department, Solicitor General Noel J. Francisco, representing the Trump administration, filed an amicus brief to the Supreme Court, surprisingly backing the (PLO) defense claims. Subsequently, the Supreme Court refused to hear the case, thereby upholding an appeals court ruling dismissing the case, saying that a lower court judge erred in concluding he had jurisdiction over the case. Was the president involved in his administration's support for the PLO? Most sources say that it was Tillerson and/or then National Security Advisor H.R. McMaster who were pulling the strings and that the president wasn't involved in the process. In any event, bad advice was given, enabling the terrorists to receive the message that terrorism is rewarded in the court of law. [18]

The policy differences between Trump and Tillerson were especially sharp when it came to the Iran issue, with the president strongly holding his ground in criticizing the Obama administration's deal with the Islamic Republic. Eventually, the policy differences at the White House became unbearable and Tillerson was replaced with firmly pro-Israel CIA Director Mike Pompeo, who was known to agree with Trump on most issues.

Trump's allies on Capitol Hill generally applauded the move, suggesting that Pompeo could help Trump deal with foreign policy challenges if only because it would be clear that he spoke for the president, when Tillerson often didn't.

"As director of the CIA, Mike has made contacts throughout the world and has come up with aggressive policies to defend our homeland. No one understands the threat posed by North Korea and Iran better than he does."

(Sen. Lindsey Graham, R-S.C.)

Standing With Allies: US Secretary of State Mike Pompeo (L) entered his new position promising to restore and strengthen the close coordination between America and its allies. In this photo, Pompeo delivers joint remarks with Israeli Prime Minister Netanyahu following meetings held in Tel Aviv at the end of April 2018.

Another key staffing improvement was the appointment in March of 2018 of former UN Ambassador John Bolton as National Security Advisor, replacing H.R. McMaster. McMaster was known to be lukewarm on Israel at best, taking the Arab position that historic Jerusalem is not a part of Israel. In planning President Trump's 2017 trip to Israel and specifically the Western Wall, McMaster had demurred when asked whether the Western Wall was part of Israel. "That's a policy decision," he said.

Coordinating the visit to the Western Wall, a first by a sitting American president, was the subject of heated debate between Israeli and American diplomats, with Israeli media reporting that a meeting descended into a shouting match after an American official said that the Western Wall "is not your territory. It's part of the West Bank." A White House statement later called those remarks "unauthorized" and

Presidential Worship: President Trump meditates at the Western Wall in Jerusalem, prior to placing a prayer in-between the stone blocks.

said they don't represent the administration's views.[19]

John Bolton as National Security Advisor is certain to project views that will be consistent with President Trump's foreign policy positions. A persuasive advocate of a proactive American foreign policy, Bolton has been known for his strong defense of Israeli sovereignty, his concern about the spread of Jihadist Islam, and his advocacy of offensive action, even including a possible preemptive strike against Iran's nuclear facilities.

Making America Secure Again: The addition of National Security Advisor John Bolton was designed to bring moral clarity to America's foreign policy.

According to Bolton, "The only logic underlying the demand for a Palestinian state is the political imperative of Israel's opponents to weaken and encircle the Jewish state, thereby minimizing its potential to establish secure and defensible borders," he wrote. "As long as Washington's diplomatic objective is the 'two-state solution' – Israel and 'Palestine' – the fundamental contradiction between this aspiration and the reality on the ground will ensure it never comes into being."

The additions of Secretary of State Pompeo and National Security Advisor Bolton were brilliant moves that brought American foreign policy in sync with President Trump's core beliefs – projecting American strength, but consistent with common sense, prudent but powerful use of the military, and unapologetic partnership with America's allies.[20]

President Trump's bold steps already taken have ushered the peace process into a new age of realism. No longer will the "land for peace" mantra be robotically recited in the Oval Office, nor will the "two-state solution" mantra be chanted in the Cabinet Room.

In April of 2018, the US State Department released its annual report on human rights violations around the world, and there was at least one discernible difference from past reports: It no longer refers to the West Bank as "occupied."

Whereas previous iterations of the Country Reports on Human Rights Practices had a section on "Israel and the Occupied Territories," this year's document refers instead to "Israel, Golan Heights, West Bank and Gaza."[21]

The West Bank should be referred to by its proper historical names – Judea and Samaria – and the Golan Heights has been a legal part of Israel for several decades. Therefore, the change in State Department policy is a very small step, but at least it's a small change in the direction of accuracy, in a government department that has long misrepresented Middle East realities. Given the positive additions to Team Trump, we can expect more positive, albeit gradual policy changes in the future.

The Trump administration has made it clear that the Palestinian Authority can't be a partner for peace negotiations, while simultaneously rewarding terrorism to the tune of $347 million a year.

This is the time for new ideas and common-sense solutions. Yes, Trump loves making deals, but like any good negotiator, he's not afraid to walk away from a bad deal, nor is he afraid to walk away from bad people, or as he might call them, "bad dudes". He's also not afraid of changing peace plans that haven't worked and/or modifying inaccurate semantics.

In the Middle East, that is not only common-sense, it's also good policy.

Chapter Nine
Big And Little Satans

"We cannot let a murderous regime continue these destabilizing activities while building dangerous missiles, and we cannot abide by an agreement if it provides cover for the eventual construction of a nuclear program. The Iran deal was one of the worst and most one-sided transactions the United States has ever entered into. Frankly, that deal is an embarrassment to the United States and I don't think you have heard the last of it..." [1]

(President Donald Trump, speaking to
the United Nations: September 2017)

President Trump had been calling the Iran deal a "disaster" long before entering the White House, but once again, he eventually backed his words with strong actions. In May of 2018, President Trump courageously announced that the United States was tearing apart its participation in the Iran nuclear deal, which had been signed in 2015 by the Obama administration, the European Union, Russia, and China with the Islamic Republic of Iran. He also signed off on the reinstitution of harsh sanctions against the Iranian regime. Immediately after his announcement, and in the months that followed, we heard the shrill cries of many on the Left, accusing the president of acting recklessly and leading America into another war. These charges of recklessness were similar to those that were also leveled at the president after his colorful exchange of insults and threats with North Korea's Kim Jong-Un. But is this indeed the reality? Is the free world truly being led by a tempestuous, moody adolescent?

To call the president reckless is, in and of itself, the irresponsible launching of verbal spears for political gain. The decision to scrap America's obligation to the Iran deal was a well-thought-out move that was the result of a long process of research and consultation.

Let's examine the reasons for the opposition to what former President Barack Obama considered to be his greatest foreign policy accomplishment, despite fierce opposition to that agreement from allies like Israel, which has undoubtedly been the single country most threatened by the fundamentalist Shiite Muslim regime. Yes, Israel has been the main target, but on the nuclear threat from Iran, Israel is no longer standing alone, as there have been some fascinating developments on this front, with several Sunni Arab nations publicly voicing their own opposition to the Iranian regime, even secretly cooperating with Israel to thwart the designs of the Islamic republic. In addition, there have been substantial street protests and a budding uprising in Iran itself against the regime.

In order to understand this very complex issue, we need some historical background to help us understand how the regime in Iran came to be such a threat to America, to Israel, to other countries in the Middle East, and to its own people.

Flashback 1978: Huge demonstrations in the streets of Teheran, Iran as the masses call for an end to the decades long rule of Mohammad Reza Pahlavi, known to all as the Shah of Iran. The demonstrations appear to have arisen as a spontaneous outburst of a longing for freedom, directed against the Shah, the autocratic ruler who had, against the wishes of the more dogmatic Islamic ideologues, increasingly modernized and westernized his country during his thirty-plus years of power. So, too, much of the opposition derived from his iron-fisted grip on what many considered to be his increasingly imperial power. Despite a parliamentary system, he was the clear and undisputed monarch and he had steered his nation in a direction that he saw as beneficial to Iran's growth and development.

As the years passed, the Shah built a strongly cooperative relationship with the United States on many levels. He had even developed a secretly cooperative economic and military relationship with Israel. While very cautious, because of the Islamic taboo not to speak positively about Israel in public, the Shah nevertheless rightly recognized Israel as the only other pro-Western nation in the Middle East and a strong American ally that he could work with. Furthermore, he understood the benefit of covert strategic cooperation with a Jewish state that had a burgeoning military industry. Israel viewed Iran as part of its strategy to develop ties with non-Arab states on the region's periphery, such as Turkey and Ethiopia. It also saw Iran as an important way station for Jews fleeing persecution in Iraq.

Furthermore, the two nations had a mutually beneficial economic relationship in trade, including the sale of Iranian oil to Israel. "Under the Shah, Israeli-Iranian ties were multi-layered and complex," said Haim Malka, a Middle East expert at the Center for Strategic and International Studies in Washington. "The Shah had a similar interest in building strategic ties with Israel, a growing military power that had a record of defeating Arab armies, though he was careful not to publicly embrace Israel too warmly," Malka said. It was "a love affair without marriage," said David Menashri, an Israeli expert on Israeli-Iranian relations, quoting an Iranian diplomat. "You don't need to have a formal contract to have a happy marriage. You are (simply) happy together." [2] Even though Iran never formally recognized Israel, the Jewish state operated a permanent delegation in Iran until the overthrow

Exporting the Islamic Revolution: After overthrowing the Shah of Iran, Ayatollah Ruhollah Khomeini made it clear that his goal was to spread his brand of Jihadist Islam around the world by supporting terrorist organizations like Hezbollah and Hamas, while encouraging terrorist activities around the world. His successor, Ayatollah Ali Khamenei, has continued and expanded the Shiite Muslim mission of "exporting the revolution".

of the Shah in 1979.

The cooperative arrangement between Israel and Iran continued unimpeded until the rebellion against the Shah's rule became a fact on the ground and there was no turning back to what once was. As the revolution grew, it soon became apparent that Iran was entering a new era, which would fundamentally change the Middle East and its web of covert and overt alliances for years to come.

Demonstrations against the Shah commenced in October 1977, developing into a widespread campaign of civil resistance that was partly secular and partly religious, and intensifying in January 1978. Between August and December 1978, strikes and demonstrations paralyzed the country. The outer face of what was then reported in the media as the Iranian pro-democracy movement, appeared to be an alliance between Islamic groups and an array of opposition groups including constitutionalist liberals – the democratic, reformist Islamic Freedom Movement of Iran, headed by Mehdi Bazargan, and the more secular National Front. They were based in the urban middle class, and wanted the Shah to adhere to the Iranian Constitution of 1906 rather than to replace him with a theocracy. Nonetheless, it soon became apparent that the driving force, indeed the more numerous,

Before the Islamic Revolution: The Shah of Iran meets with US President Jimmy Carter in 1977.

better organized, and cohesive catalyst behind the revolution was the Shiite Muslim movement of Ayatollah Ruhollah Khomeini.

Eventually, succumbing to the pressure of the revolution while simultaneously battling an advanced stage of cancer, the Shah left Iran for exile on January 16, 1979 as the last Persian monarch. Ayatollah Khomeini returned to Tehran two weeks later to a rousing welcome by several million Iranians. The royal reign collapsed on February 11, 1979.

Iran voted by national referendum to become an Islamic Republic on April 1, 1979, and to approve a new democratic-theocratic hybrid constitution whereby Khomeini became Supreme Leader of the country in December 1979.[3]

The rise to power of the Islamic ideologues in Iran almost immediately led to a flexing of muscles and a crisis with the United States, during which 52 Americans were held hostage for 444 days from November 4, 1979, to January 20, 1981, after a group of Islamic students and militants took over the American Embassy in Tehran in a show of support for the Iranian Revolution and anger towards "the Great Satan" ("The Little Satan" in their semantics being Israel).[4]

This entire process was viewed helplessly from abroad by American President Jimmy Carter, whose confusing approach to the Shah's rule probably hastened the monarch's downfall. As we discussed earlier, when the Shah visited the White House in November 1977, he was the recipient of public expressions of support from the president, but he was later chastised in private meetings by Carter for his spotty human rights record. The Shah was strongly urged to consider reaching out to dissident groups and "easing off" on police actions against them.[5] This pressure was something new to the Shah and the timing of Carter's reprimand couldn't have been worse for the embattled Persian leader, who was already in a fight for both personal and political survival. Likewise, Carter's demand not to repress the revolution, an implied message of reduced American support for the Shah, would soon be interpreted as weakness by the Ayatollah and his cohorts.

The Islamic theocracy has been in power in Iran ever since and has, undisputedly, been the most consistent supporter of Islamic terrorism in the Middle East and throughout the world, mostly of the Shiite variety. Their most infamous patron is Hezbollah, which currently has 150,000 rockets, including a number of long range Iranian-made missiles capable of striking Israeli cities from north to south,[6] and they have also heavily funded the predominantly Sunni Hamas terrorist organization, which is based in Gaza, but is active in other parts of Israel, as well. Furthermore, the regime has been quite transparent about its intention to export that revolution to the free world.

We shall export our revolution to the whole world. Until the cry ... There is no god but Allah ... resounds over the whole world, there will be struggle.[7]

(Ayatollah Ruhollah Khomeini, 1979)

Ronald Reagan's campaign message of peace through American military strength and toughness contrasted sharply with Jimmy Carter's weak image in the eyes of the world, and especially Iran. Sadly, the Iran hostage crisis symbolized America's decline, both economically and militarily. Most Americans who lived through the Carter years remember his depressing "Crisis of Confidence" speech to the nation, in which he bemoaned the loss of optimism in America under his leadership. Reagan sought to turn that around by inspiring America again. Similar to Trump-Pence 2016, Reagan's campaign slogan was "Let's Make America Great Again", restoring a sense of optimism that the Carter years had diminished. Nonetheless, nobody expected the turnaround to happen so quickly.

Whether the timing was directly related to Reagan's rise to power or not, the fact is that the hostages were released on January 20, 1981, as Reagan was sworn in as President of the United States. On that very day, at the moment President Reagan completed his 20-minute inaugural address after being sworn in, the 52 American hostages were handed over to US personnel.[8]

Shortly thereafter, Iraq invaded Iran in September 1980, triggering a bitter eight-year war which destabilized the region and devastated both countries. Iraqi leader Saddam Hussein claimed as a reason for the invasion a territorial dispute over the Shatt al-Arab, the waterway which forms the boundary between the two countries. However, the conflict was rooted in regional rivalry. Saddam Hussein felt directly threatened by the Islamic revolution which had brought Ayatollah Khomeini to power in Iran the year before. The Ayatollah, for his part, saw Saddam as a brutal Sunni tyrant oppressing his country's Shia majority, and did not disguise his desire to see him toppled.

Thus, for Saddam Hussein, the war's purpose was pre-

Death to Israel, Death to America: Iran's supreme religious leader Ayatollah Ali Khamenei, just as extreme as his predecessor.

emptive: to overthrow the Khomeini regime before that regime could overthrow him.[9]

Neither side succeeded and the war lasted for eight years, with hundreds of thousands of lives lost and no conclusive results.

Ayatollah Khomeini died in 1989, but during the next two decades, Iran slowly rebuilt itself as a regional power under the leadership of his successor Ayatollah Khamenei, who also has ruled Iran with an iron fist. Iran watched gleefully from the sidelines, as the George HW Bush administration focused on fighting Iraq, then some years later, as Bush the son finished the job in the second war against Iraq.

After Saddam Hussein suffered that bitter defeat at the hands of the Bush administration and its allies, Iraq's military power greatly decreased and the country disintegrated into fierce ethnic rivalries between Shiites, Sunnis, and Kurds.

Meanwhile, Ayatollah Khamenei exploited the consequential regional power vacuum to greatly expand Iran's clout as a regional player, using Iran's vast oil and gas wealth to accomplish two primary nefarious goals:

- To develop a nuclear bomb and the weapons to go with it.

- To fulfill Ayatollah Khomeini's mission to "export the Islamic revolution" by supporting Islamic terrorist organizations and allies in the Middle East and elsewhere.

According to a report by the Council on Foreign Relations, as of 2010, Iran had succeeded way beyond belief in accomplishing those two goals:

The US State Department considers Iran the world's "most active state sponsor of terrorism." US officials say Iran provides funding, weapons, training, and sanctuary to numerous terrorist groups – most notably in Iraq, Afghanistan, and Lebanon – posing a security concern to the international community. Iran's declarations that it has successfully enriched uranium and developed new missile technology have heightened alarm in the United States and other countries that the Islamic Republic might transfer weapons of mass destruction to militants or armed groups. Iran's leaders, who deny allegations they support terrorism ... assert their rights under an international treaty to pursue nuclear power and insist their efforts are for peaceful purposes.[10]

Nukes for peaceful purposes? A country with the third largest oil reserves in the world and the second largest gas reserves in the world needs nuclear energy for peaceful purposes?

The rise of Iran as the primary state sponsor of Islamic

terrorism and as a potential nuclear power occurred on the watches of three American presidents, long before Obama was elected in 2008. The truth be told, as dangerous as the 2015 Iran nuclear deal was, the previous administrations of Bush I, Clinton, and Bush II were totally irresponsible for letting it get to this point. It's not like the ayatollahs had ever hid their evil intentions:

"It is the mission of the Islamic Republic of Iran to erase Israel from the map of the region." [11]

(Ayatollah Ali Khamenei, 2001)

"Our people say 'Death to America,' and this is like saying 'I seek God's refuge from the accursed Satan,' which is recited before any chapter of the Koran, even before 'In the name of Allah the Compassionate, the Merciful.' Why is this? So the believer will never forget, even for a moment, the presence of Satan. So he will never forget, even for a moment, that Satan is ready to attack him and to destroy his spiritual shield and his faith ... The saying "Death to America" is for this purpose." [12]

(Ayatollah Ali Khamenei, 2005)

The Iran regime invested many billions of dollars in its nuclear program over several decades, building nuclear research and development centers in difficult to reach underground bunkers, thereby establishing a formidable infrastructure that nuclear inspectors could be easily denied access to. Furthermore, threatened countries like Israel, the United States, or certain Sunni Muslim countries would find it nearly impossible to penetrate such a comprehensive system.

Through the years, it was reported that the Israeli government seriously considered planning a pre-emptive strike, but for a variety of internal and external reasons, it never materialized. It has been said that one of the main

Pushed For A Deal At All Costs: US Secretary of State John Kerry (L-Front) meets with Iranian Foreign Minister Javad Zarif and Dr. Ali Akbar Salehi, the Vice President of Iran for Atomic Energy and President of the Atomic Energy Organization of Iran. Kerry claimed that "Iran deserves the benefits" of its nuclear deal.

reasons for the Obama administration's mad race, along with its European partners, to finalize the Iran deal was to prevent Israel from launching such an attack.

The Obama administration was determined to sign the Iran nuclear deal, despite the vehement, persistent opposition of Israel Prime Minister Benjamin Netanyahu. Netanyahu was quite vocal in speaking out about his objections to the deal, even appearing before the full Congress at the invitation of the GOP House Speaker John Boehner to voice his objections to and urge the congress to vote against "a bad deal". While some of the Israeli Left were perturbed that Netanyahu made a high profile speech to Congress just two weeks before the Israeli elections, the content of very public objections to the deal were backed by a rare wall-to-wall opposition to the deal from all across the Israeli political spectrum.

Nonetheless, Obama, his Secretary of State John Kerry,

and the rest of his foreign policy team were not to be deterred. On July 14, 2015, the Iran nuclear deal, officially called the Joint Comprehensive Plan of Action, was signed by Iran, the P5+1 (the five permanent members of the United Nations Security Council – China, France, Russia, United Kingdom, United States – plus Germany) and the European Union. [13]

James Jay Carafano, a national security and foreign policy expert, wrote a clear and succinct critique of the deal that the Obama administration seemed obsessed with signing at all costs.

Here he lists the four most dangerous problems with the deal:

- The whole neighborhood will race to go nuclear. The number-one concern with the way this deal was structured was that it was bound to accelerate nuclear proliferation. Iran has violated its obligations under the Nuclear Nonproliferation Treaty (NPT) and repeatedly thumbed its nose at oversight from the International Atomic Energy Agency (IAEA). Yet it winds up getting a great deal under the agreement – better, in fact, than the deal the United States gives its friends and allies through the 123 Civil Nuclear Agreements. If regional powers like Turkey, Egypt and Saudi Arabia believe that the likelihood of Iran getting a weapon is undiminished and the penalty for becoming a nuclear breakout power is plummeting, then the deterrent for them to cross the nuclear threshold drops as well.

- Tehran gets to keep its vast nuclear infrastructure and its missile program. Other regional powers are likely to race to nuclear, in part because the deal does nothing to scuttle Iran's plans to build a weapon. The administration's pitch is that the deal slows down

Iran's program, leaving plenty of time for "early warning" of a nuclear breakout. That's cold comfort for Tehran's neighbors. What's freaked them out is knowing that Iran will eventually put a nuclear warhead on a missile – and this deal won't stop that. Further, even if the administration does receive early warning (a dubious promise at best), it has never indicated what – if anything – it would do about it. Indeed, these promises from Iran only confirm the obvious: that the regime definitely has nuclear-weapons ambitions. After all, why have a massive ballistic-missile program and secret military nuclear facilities if the plan isn't to build nuclear weapons?

- Sanctions relief will make the region far less safe. People will argue the numbers, but the sanctions relief and the renewed ability to sell more oil on the open market could wind up bringing $300-400 billion into the Iranian economy. As in any thriving kleptocracy, that money will be funneled through the hands of the regime, whose leaders will use it to tighten their grip on the Iranian people and fund the most aggressive and destabilizing foreign policy outside of ISIS. Essentially, the deal will pay for undermining US policy and interests throughout the region.

- The deal is temporary, by design. Even the White House doesn't claim it will permanently keep Iran from getting a bomb. So, what's the point? Mr. Obama can't even guarantee it will outlive his presidency. After a couple of years of cashing in on sanctions relief, Tehran might just walk away.

The (Obama) Oval Office insists that there are only two choices:

this deal or war. But the choices are neither that limited, nor that simple. This deal is not the antidote to war. Rather, it makes increased conflict all the more likely, as a newly enriched and emboldened Iran increases its destabilizing activities throughout the region and its threatened neighbors pursue more extreme measures for self-preservation." [14]

Since the deal was signed, thereby freeing up billions of dollars that were to be transferred, either immediately or at a later date, into Iranian hands, the regime has significantly increased its financial support for two of the largest terror groups in the region that have now become major political players, Hezbollah and Hamas. Understanding that many billions of dollars would soon be flowing into the country in the coming years as a result of the removal of sanctions, the Iranian government boosted its already substantial support for those two terrorist organizations, which are ensconced on Israel's northern and southern borders, respectively.

This support, for example, has enabled Hezbollah to obtain highly developed new armaments, including advanced technologies that many militaries around the world would envy. Al-Rai, a Kuwaiti newspaper, reported that Hezbollah has received all the advanced weaponry that Syria has obtained from the Russians. The report cited a security source involved in the fighting in Zabadani, on the Syria-Lebanon border, where Hezbollah is fighting the al-Nusra Front, the Islamic State, and other groups. It is evidently the growing Iranian financial support that is enabling the Lebanese Shiite militia to purchase advanced weapons, including ones that were hitherto outside of its reach. [15]

Hezbollah's domination of Lebanon, which actually means Iran's domination of Lebanon, recently caused Lebanese Prime Minister, Saad Hariri, to temporarily resign, and flee to Saudi Arabia. Hariri, denouncing Hezbollah and its Iranian backers, said he feared for his life. Hariri has good reason to be afraid of Hezbollah, the powerful Shiite terror group and Iranian proxy that effectively controls Lebanon.

Indications show that Iran and Hezbollah are also planning to extend their control to the Gaza Strip. Iran already provides Hamas with financial and military aid. It is precisely the support of Iran that has enabled Hamas to hold power in the Gaza Strip for the past twelve years. It is also thanks to Iran that Hamas and Palestinian Islamic Jihad, another major terror group in the Gaza Strip, are in possession of thousands of missiles and rockets. It is (also) Iranian money that allows Hamas and Islamic Jihad to continue digging terror tunnels under the border with Israel. [16]

Hamas, which is now once again an integral partner in the ruling Palestinian Authority, has increased its influence over Mahmoud Abbas, the chairman of the Palestinian quasi-government and the Fatah terrorist organization. The Fatah-Hamas-Hezbollah axis of power is heavily funded by Teheran, thereby creating great instability in the Middle East and substantially increasing the possibility of a multi-front war along Israel's borders, in Syria, in Lebanon, and perhaps beyond.

Which brings us to the present. In his first year in office, President Trump decertified the Iran deal, setting the stage for a showdown. What it meant was that the president confirmed that the Iran deal as signed was not in the security interests of the United States. In essence, he threw it back into the hands of Congress and the European partners, demanding that they make the necessary changes in the deal that would have made it in the American interest not to abrogate.

"We will not continue down a path whose predictable conclusion is more violence, more terror, and the very real threat of Iran's nuclear breakout," he said in a speech at the White House. "In the event

we are not able to reach a solution working with Congress and our allies, then the agreement will be terminated. It is under continuous review, and our participation can be canceled by me, as president, at any time." [17]

What changes were suggested? Firstly, Congress could have chosen to pull out of the deal, but then Secretary of State Rex Tillerson said the administration would advise it instead to establish guidelines under which the US could automatically re-impose sanctions: trigger points, he called them. The Trump administration hoped to broaden Iran policy beyond the nuclear deal. This, said Tillerson, would have included sanctioning members of the powerful Islamic Revolutionary Guards (IRGC) force for supporting militant groups and terrorist activities. Among the changes it sought was the end to the "sunset" clauses in the deal, which saw restrictions on Iran's nuclear enrichment program lifted after 2025, greater access to inspect nuclear sites, and the inclusion of Iran's ballistic missile program.

Efforts would be made to deny funding for the Iranian government and the IRGC's "malign activities" and counter threats from ballistic missiles "and other asymmetric weapons".[18] President Trump's firmness in opposing Iran's aggressiveness and his determination to prevent them from acquiring nuclear capability was, at least from the Israeli viewpoint, a refreshing departure from Obama's obsequious behavior towards the Islamic Republic. Obviously, Iran's Rouhani shared a slightly different perspective:

"Today, the president of America has created conditions where Iran is more united than ever. Today, those who oppose the nuclear deal, and those who support it, are side by side. We all have one voice," Iran's President Hassan Rouhani said, in response to the Iran deal's decertification.[19]

But are the Iranians really united? In late December into early January 2018, tens of thousands of protestors took to the streets in at least ten different cities of Iran, complaining about economic hardships and a corrupt leadership, with some claiming that the protests questioned the very foundations of the Islamic Republic.

Tehran member of parliament Mahmoud Sadeghi said that 3,700 people had been arrested, including 40 to 68 students, in six days of protests. The number is far higher than the 450 people Iranian authorities previously said were detained. US officials had put the number held at 1,000. [20]

At least 21 people were killed by IRGC security forces in a brutal crackdown on the protestors, with several killed in custody. The regime quickly shut down social media and other media to quell any further protests, as well as the reports of further protests. Nonetheless, there have been sporadic reports of continuing protests throughout Iran well into 2018.

Unlike President Obama during similar protests in 2009, President Trump tweeted strong encouragement for the protests. His support was appreciated, but apparently it wasn't enough when faced with a brutal, fanatical dictatorship.

Barring some unforeseen major internal rebellion in the near future, the Iran nuclear issue will continue to be at the top of the foreign policy agenda, and it could well lead to a necessary military conflict. Here in Israel, we have almost learned the sad reality that putting our heads in the Middle East sand doesn't ever make the problem go away. It's never pleasant, but at some point, evil has to be confronted and mercilessly destroyed.

"Those who are kind to the cruel are destined to be cruel to the kind."
(Midrash Yalkut Shimoni)

That message from Jewish wisdom was also emphasized, in his own words, by the great British statesman, Winston

Heir to the Throne Making Waves: Crown Prince Mohammed bin Salman, of Saudi Arabia, seen here with President Trump, has been charting a new path for his kingdom, by relaxing strict Islamic social norms, speaking out against Iran, and most significantly, forming an unwritten alliance with the Jewish state. Will this trend continue?

Churchill, who urged hesitant world leaders to fight the necessary all-out war against the Nazis in World War II. It is also a message that, ironically, has been delivered recently by none other than the young, charismatic Crown Prince Mohammed bin Salman, of Saudi Arabia, who, in an April 2018 interview with *The Atlantic*, not only affirmed Israel's right to exist – itself a bit of a revolution in the Islamic world, but harshly criticized former President Obama's Iran policy, thereby signaling support for President Trump's Middle East agenda, as well as slightly removing the symbolic veil that has hidden the Saudi kingdom's budding alliance with Israel.

"Hitler didn't do what the supreme leader (of Iran) is trying to do," the crown prince told *The Atlantic*.

"Hitler tried to conquer Europe. This is bad. But the

supreme leader is trying to conquer the world. He believes he owns the world. They are both evil guys. He is the Hitler of the Middle East. In the 1920s and 1930s, no one saw Hitler as a danger. Only a few people. Until it happened." [21]

Does this mean that Saudi Arabia is becoming a true friend of Israel? Highly unlikely. The moderate statements towards rapprochement with Israel seem to be symptomatic of "My enemy's enemy is my friend". What is developing is a marriage of convenience based on Saudi Arabia's fear of Shiite Iran, but it's very premature, and probably foolish, to pull out the champagne.[22]

Unlike the United States and Israel, which have a friendship based on shared values, most alliances, whether

Iran Lied: Prime Minister Netanyahu exposes the ongoing lies and deception, through which the Iranian regimes shielded its nuclear research and development program from international inspection. These 100,000 files, captured by the Israeli Mossad intelligence agency, revealed that Iran has been in flagrant violation of the nuclear deal that it had signed with the Obama administration, along with the EU, Russia, and China.

long or short-term, are based on shared interests, and the Israel-Saudi relationship is no exception. Despite the Crown Prince's concerns, and despite his kingdom's substantial arsenal of American weapons, there is no way that the Saudis would take on Iran themselves. The Saudis need Israel to stop the Iranian tsunami. If some economic cooperation and even a little real friendship comes out of that, it can only be good.

On May 8, 2018, after hearing about the Israeli Mossad intelligence agency's incredible capture of 100,000 files revealing years of Iranian lies, as well as its non-compliance with the terms of the nuclear deal, President Trump announced that the United States was immediately pulling out of the deal and reimposing harsh sanctions on the Iranian regime and those who cooperate with the Iranian regime.

Some highlights from President Trump's speech:

"The Iranian regime is the leading state sponsor of terror. It exports dangerous missiles, fuels conflicts across the Middle East, and supports terrorist proxies and militias such as Hezbollah, Hamas, the Taliban and al-Qaeda.

"In the years since the deal was reached, Iran's military budget has grown by almost 40%, while its economy is doing very badly. After the sanctions were lifted, the dictatorship used its new funds to build nuclear-capable missiles, support terrorism, and cause havoc throughout the Middle East and beyond.

"The agreement was so poorly negotiated that even if Iran fully complies, the regime can still be on the verge of a nuclear breakout in just a short period of time. The deal's sunset provisions are totally unacceptable. If I allowed this deal to stand, there would soon be a nuclear arms race in the Middle East. Everyone would want their weapons ready by the time Iran had theirs.

"Making matters worse, the deal's inspection provisions lack adequate mechanisms to prevent, detect, and punish cheating, and don't even have the unqualified right to inspect many important locations, including military facilities.

"Not only does the deal fail to halt Iran's nuclear ambitions, but it also fails to address the regime's development of ballistic missiles that could deliver nuclear warheads.

"The Iran deal is defective at its core. If we do nothing, we know exactly what will happen. In just a short period of time, the world's leading state sponsor of terror will be on the cusp of acquiring the world's most dangerous weapons.

"Therefore, I am announcing today that the United States will withdraw from the Iran nuclear deal.

"In a few moments, I will sign a presidential memorandum to begin reinstating US nuclear sanctions on the Iranian regime. We will be instituting the highest level of economic sanction. Any nation that helps Iran in its quest for nuclear

Making America Tough Again: President Trump holds up a new presidential memorandum that reinstated nuclear sanctions on the Iranian regime.

weapons could also be strongly sanctioned by the United States.

"America will not be held hostage to nuclear blackmail. We will not allow American cities to be threatened with destruction. And we will not allow a regime that chants 'Death to America' to gain access to the most deadly weapons on Earth." [23]

President Trump has kept his word. America is out. The Europeans remain in the deal, but without the partnership of the United States, the deal is effectively doomed. Even though Trump held out the prospect of an eventual modified deal, Iran isn't biting. Unlike North Korea, which badly wants peace with South Korea and to retain power, even at the expense of its nuclear program, for Iran there is no such reckoning.

We must remember that the Ayatollahs are Shiite Muslim radicals, fanatical ideologues who will stop at nothing to achieve Jihad, holy war, against their enemies. Their main swords are aimed at "the Big Satan" and the "Little Satan", but their targets include, as well, the more moderate Sunni Muslim nations, such as Saudi Arabia.

So, the obvious question that will be flooding the Trump-hating media will be, "Are we heading to war?", but the more rational question would be and should be, "What are the actual ramifications of the American exit?"

To say that war is not a risk would be inaccurate, but strengthening a vicious enemy like the Iranian regime and paving its way to a nuclear bomb and the ability to deliver it would be far more dangerous, a form of near-surrender. The renewal of harsh economic sanctions on Iran can help to weaken the regime and will provide moral support to the growing opposition in Iran. Such steps will set the stage for the growing conflict between Israel and Iran, which has already begun.

The conflict with Iran has recently entered a new, more

dangerous phase, in which Iran and Israel are in direct military conflict, at this point in Syria, as Iran attempts to establish bases along Israel's northern border. In April of 2018, after Prime Minister Netanyahu consulted with President Trump, the Israeli military struck hard at an advanced Iranian air-defense system at the T-4 airbase in Homs, Syria. Seven Iranian personnel were killed in the early morning strike. Netanyahu ordered the strike on the newly arrived anti-aircraft battery to prevent Iranian forces from using it against Israeli warplanes carrying out increasing numbers of operations in Syria.[24]

Since then, there have been more strikes on Iranian military bases in Syria, as Israel fought back against Iranian efforts to establish itself militarily on Israel's northern border.

On May 9, 2018, after Iran fired 20 rockets in the direction of the Israeli Golan Heights, the Israel Defense Forces deployed fighter jets and used missiles to strike dozens of Iranian targets in Syria, including military compounds, intelligence/logistics centers, munitions warehouses, and listening posts. The strikes were Israel's largest air operation in Syria since the 1973 Yom Kippur War.

The worldwide response was revealing, European leaders were ambivalent, but the Trump administration led the way with its unequivocal support for the Israeli operation:

"The United States condemns the Iranian regime's provocative rocket attack from Syria against Israeli citizens, and we strongly support Israel's right to act in self-defense," Press Secretary Sarah Sanders said in a statement. "The Iranian regime's deployment into Syria of offensive rocket and missile systems aimed at Israel is an unacceptable and highly dangerous development for the entire Middle East." [25]

While France and Russia urged calm, the UK and

Germany spoke up for Israel, with the spokesperson for British Prime Minister Theresa May launching an unusually strong defense of the Jewish state.[26]

"We condemn Iran's attack on Israel. Israel has every right to defend itself ... We call on Iran to refrain from any further attacks and for calm on all sides. We call on Russia to use its influence in Syria to prevent further Iranian attacks."
(United Kingdom)

"We are deeply concerned by reports about last night's Iranian rocket attacks on Israeli army outposts ... These attacks are a severe provocation that we most strongly condemn. We have always emphasized that Israel has a the right to defend itself."
(German Foreign Ministry)

If history is any guide, we can expect that as the Israel-Iran conflict heats up further, the European support for Israel will lessen, with the French-Russian calls for calm spreading to others in the European Union. After the American withdrawal and reimposition of harsh sanctions on Iran, all of these countries remain signatories in the Iran nuclear deal and don't want to see their business ties with Iran blow up in smoke. It's also important to remember that Russia holds the key to calming this particular conflict. The Iranian military presence in Syria can end in a day if Russia ends its ambivalent patronage of that presence.

Perhaps the most revealing response to the Israeli air strikes came from Khalid Bin Ahmed Al Khalifa, the Foreign Minister of the Gulf Arab state Bahrain, who tweeted support for Israel and endorsed the Jewish state's right to self-defense:

"As long as Iran has breached the status quo in the region and invaded countries with its forces and missiles, so any state in the region, including Israel, is entitled to defend itself by destroying sources of danger."[27]

Bahrain, a majority Sunni Muslim nation and close ally of Saudi Arabia, has a long-standing rivalry with Iran, following the failed attempt by Iranian-backed terrorists to overthrow the Bahrain government in 1981. Furthermore, and more significant, as with the Saudis, the fear of Iran has led to carefully discreet cooperation with Israel, but now they are starting to go public with their support, and that is, indeed, remarkable.

Can this be the harbinger of a coming Israeli air strike into the heart of Iran's nuclear program, even deep into Iran itself? According to a former Israel Air Force pilot, who took part in the destruction of Iraq's nuclear reactor in 1981, Israel is fully capable of successfully striking Iran:

"If the decision is taken by the political echelon, the air force pilots and planes are capable of doing it," Brig.-Gen. (res.) Amir Nachumi said.

Nachumi led one of two formations of four aircraft each that destroyed the (Iraqi) Osirak nuclear reactor near Baghdad in 1981.

He also cited the more recent Israeli attack against the Syrian nuclear reactor (in Deir al-Zor in 2007) as further proof of Israeli air capability.

According to Nachumi, the (successful) operations in Iraq and Syria were long-range missions carried out by F-15s and F-16s that were "capable of carrying them out with no aerial refueling."

The distance between Israel and Iran "makes it more complicated" than the strikes on Iraq and Syria, he said, acknowledging the obstacles which could arise in attacking the Islamic Republic's nuclear facilities. Nonetheless, "Even though Syria is closer to us distance-wise, the complications are no less than what we are expecting if we go to Iran," he said.

"But I am sure that the (Israeli) air force of today – which is by far more developed and advanced with technology that we did not have in 1981 – is capable of doing it."

In December, the IAF became the first air force outside the United States to declare initial operational capability of its F-35 stealth fighter jets. The (Israeli-upgraded) Adir version of the world's most advanced and expensive fighter jet was designed to Israel's specifications and is embedded with Israeli-made electronic warfare pods as well as Israeli weaponry and is expected to be used for long-range missions.[28]

The anti-Ayatollah protests in Iran have continued, and the overthrow of the deranged Islamic regime by pro-Western elements could actually happen, although it's not likely. No one should doubt the ruthlessness of the regime in repressing all internal opposition, and even if an opposition rebellion were to succeed, there is no guarantee that it would be pro-Western.

Barring such a relatively peaceful resolution to the problem of Iranian nuclear weapons and other aggressions, the only long-term solution may be military. If history is any indication, Israel will not wait for full Iranian nuclear capability. Unless the Islamic Republic strikes first, an Israeli preemptive strike is probably inevitable. Most likely scenario? A massive Israeli air strike on Iran with passive American military and political support, and the use of Saudi air space. Stay tuned…

Chapter Ten

Eleven Suggestions For Trump (From The Jews)

"Who is wise? One who learns from every person."

(Ethics of the Fathers 4:1)

"It is insufficient that you be a servant for Me to (only) raise up the tribes of Jacob and to restore the ruins of Israel; I will make you a light unto the nations..."

(Isaiah 2:3)

Through nearly two thousand years of exile from the Land of Israel, we Jews have learned to survive, but also to thrive in the most challenging of circumstances. In each country that we lived in, we learned new survival skills, new creative skills, and ways to adjust to new situations. Now that we are back in our natural habitat, we can put those skills to use in new ways. We can also share those skills and knowledge, not to mention the obvious moral lessons acquired from the Almighty, with our genuine friends around the world.

"Why is Israel like a dove? Other birds, when tired, rest on a branch; but when the dove tires, she rests one wing and flies with the other."

(Midrash Genesis Rabbah 39:10)

The Jewish knowledge and the creative, enterprising spirit has been acquired through adversity, but the ultimate source all along has been Torah and Jewish values. As an American-Israeli Jew, who grew up in Brooklyn, but has been living in

Israel since 1992, I have gotten to see and experience both sides, or every side, of the multi-faceted Jewish coin, from passionate liberalism to passionate Orthodoxy to passionate Zionism.

There is no real Judaism without passion, but not everything that Jews are passionate about is consistent with Judaism. There is certainly room for differences, but not for a misrepresentation of Jewish values.

The traditional family in Judaism may seem old-fashioned and is often ridiculed by some with an extreme liberal agenda seeking to rewrite gender biology in their own image of choice – be it male, female, trans, or gender-neutral. The Union for Reform Judaism – the congregational arm of the movement in the United States – has a toolkit for synagogues that includes a section on how to tailor *b'nei mitzvah* ceremonies to align with the child's gender identity, said Rabbi Leora Kaye, program director.

"What we're seeing now is that there are families and there are congregations that are very open to exploring with the kids that are becoming bar and bat mitzvah how they want to be identified," Kaye told JTA.[1]

Choosing one's own gender and gender-neutrality are now Jewish values? From where in the Torah, the Talmud, and the commentaries does this come? Perhaps the Bar/Bat Mitzvah child's spiritually uplifting Torah speech will be about gender choice? Will the Jewish values in that speech be based on Judaism or perhaps on the extreme liberal definitions of sexual identity? In Judaism, there is a great deal of freedom and room for differences of opinion, but there are also standards that are based on the Torah of Israel. Pretending that those standards don't exist and then calling the resultant chaos and hedonism "Judaism" is intellectually dishonest.

Going back to the topic of Israel and the so-called peace process, the misunderstanding of Jewish values is especially pronounced and even extends to the casual abandonment of Israel's ancestral heartland. Despite a clear shift in both Israeli and US policy on the issue, AIPAC (American Israel Public Affairs Committee) CEO Howard Kohr, speaking at the organization's 2018 conference, urged Israel and the Palestinian Authority to return to the negotiating table and secure an agreement paving the way for the establishment of a Palestinian state.

"We must all work toward that future: two states for two peoples," said Kohr. "One Jewish with secure and defensible borders, and one Palestinian with its own flag and its own future. Today that dream seems remote. This is tragic."

Kohr lamented the present diplomatic impasse, warning that the failure to achieve a two-state solution leaves Israel vulnerable.[2]

Time for a fact and reality check, which can be easily confirmed by speaking to Mahmoud Abbas of the Palestinian Authority. The Palestinians, at a very minimum, expect to build their independent state in at least 90% of Samaria and Judea, with their capital in Jerusalem. However, the great Jewish leader, Joshua, upon establishing Shiloh as the first capital of ancient Israel in the heart of Samaria, said the following words to the Israelites:

"How long will you hesitate, to come and take possession of the land that the Lord, God of your fathers has given you?"
(Joshua 18:3)

To Howard Kohr, these words are apparently not so important, but for a Jew whose Jewish values and common sense come from the sources of Judaism, the biblical imperatives about the Land of Israel are critical to Israel's long-term survival.

Does Kohr's prescription for Israel's survival make Jewish sense? Do Jewish values actually dictate that Israel withdraw from the heartland of Judea and Samaria that God commanded us to possess? Furthermore, there is a Jewish value called *Pikuach Nefesh* (the saving of a life). Would we actually save Jewish lives by placing a sovereign Palestinian state run by Hamas and Fatah terrorists on the Samarian mountain peaks overlooking Ben Gurion International Airport and just nine miles from its runways?

This perversion of Jewish values even extends to Jerusalem, Israel's eternal capital and the powerful symbol of Israel's full return to the Land of Israel in fulfillment of biblical prophecy. When Reform rabbis criticized President Trump for declaring American recognition of Jerusalem as Israel's capital, calling his decision "ill-timed" because it would "exacerbate the conflict", one has to wonder on what Jewish values they have based their response to the president's declaration. After the many centuries of Jewish prayers and tears that have been shed over Jerusalem, and after years of demanding that the same basic respect given to rogue nations like Cuba and Iran be given to Israel, they refer to Trump's recognition as "ill-timed"? [3]

How sad that these "rabbis" are the shepherds leading the sheep! Furthermore, when they complain that President Trump's proposed restrictions on immigration from Muslim/terror dominated countries are contrary to Jewish values, I have to wonder what values they are referring to. Is the protection of innocent American lives somehow contrary to Jewish values?

Nancy Matlin is a proud American Jew who grew up at a Conservative temple in California but recently stopped paying temple dues. "Our Jewish community," she explained, "changed during the Obama years and after the election of Donald Trump. Instead of teaching our children and young adults the history of Israel and Zionism, the community now focuses a lot of its energy on connections to the Muslim community, and on a form of *Tikun Olam* (repairing the world) to help everyone, *except* Jews and Israel. The local rabbi invited the leadership of a Muslim mosque to a Passover Seder, so that they could teach the Jewish children about Islam. Even so, when Imam Ammar Shahin, the young imam (Muslim religious leader) in the neighboring town of Davis, called for the murder of Jews, none of those local rabbis or their imam friends publicly criticized it. The final straw was the failure of the Reform and Conservative rabbis to oppose Obama's nuclear deal with Iran, opting instead to 'promote meaningful dialogue'. To me, this was cowardice in the face of a clear and present danger to Israel and the Jewish people." [4]

Perhaps the Jewish liberal rabbis could ask whether their Muslim colleagues believe in Jihad (holy war against non-Muslims) or whether they believe in Islamic Sharia law that permits polygamy and wife-beating, doesn't permit freedom of worship for other religions, and calls for the murder of a Muslim who leaves Islam? Perhaps they could also ask whether their Muslim friends would condemn Hamas or whether they support the right of Israel to exist as a Jewish state. Sadly, the American Muslim leadership is exploiting these naive Jews who apparently have their Jewish values confused with a very misguided, self-destructive version of bleeding-heart liberalism.

President Trump was elected to the leadership of a country that is hurting in many ways, but he has brought to the White House a refreshingly non-dogmatic approach that served him well in the world of business. He, too, is determined and passionate about the things he believes in strongly, but he is also open to new ideas that might work. With that constructive approach to problem-solving, he has begun a bold process to free up the American economy from excessive regulation and make America a great place to invest and to grow a business. On the foreign policy front, he has taken action to strengthen America's damaged ties with its allies. However, the social divisions, the breakdown of the American family, the random crime in schools and other public spaces, along with the ongoing Islamic terror threat and nuclear threats from serious enemies – all are challenges that still need to be met, and it won't be easy, especially after the Obama years, when these problems only got worse.

Solutions to all of these challenges can be found, and many of them are in the value system of the people that brought the Bible to the world. Judaism is, indeed, filled with a rich value system, mainly rooted in the Torah, the Bible of Israel, along with the Talmud, the oral tradition passed down from Mount Sinai, and a vast array of commentaries about those texts and other related texts. Christianity, which is still the dominant religion in the United States, is actually an outgrowth of Judaism. In fact, Jesus was a Jew who lived only in the Land of Israel and most of his own teachings came from Judaism, and therefore, it's a good idea for Americans to look to Israel and to real Jewish values, to find some common-sense solutions that hopefully, people can agree on.

• Restoring God To America

"Love the Lord your God with all your heart, with all your soul, and with all your might."
(Deuteronomy 6:5)

As we discussed in chapter one, God was once front and center in American life and particularly, in American education. The intense efforts of political atheists and misguided liberals in Hollywood to remove God and the biblical heritage from the public sphere has led to a decrease in religious observance in the past few decades. This has created a vacuum in America that has correlated with a parallel sharp increase in random crime and suicide rates. In Israel, on the other hand, people have been becoming more religiously observant, the Jewish birth rate is increasing in all segments of the population, and suicide rates are way down, while surveys show that people are happy with their lives, especially those who feel connected to God and Jewish tradition.[5]

"I am profitably engaged in reading the Bible. Take all of this book upon reason that you can, and the balance by faith, and you will live and die a better man." [6]

(Abraham Lincoln)

As the founders of America have attested to, and as religious Jews have always known, strong connection to biblical teachings and the humbling of ourselves to the Creator provide a solid framework for a healthy life and a constant effort at self-improvement. Religious liberty should be defended against the assault of those who want to undo America's Judeo-Christian foundations, while free access to sound moral teachings should be encouraged.

- ## Strengthen The American Family

"Honor your father and your mother, that your days may be long in the land that the Lord your God is giving you."

(Exodus 20:12)

"Teach them to your children. Talk about them when you sit at home and when you are on the road, when you are going to bed and when you are getting up."

(Deuteronomy 11:19)

About thirty-five years ago, I taught in an inner-city school in Brooklyn. Of my twenty-seven students, only seven had "fathers who they see every week". The breakdown of the traditional American family of mother, father, and children is one of the great tragedies of modern American life. Yes, I know, there are some very successful single-parent families led by a very strong single parent, but I would guess that most single parents would agree that it's not the ideal, in which both parents complement each other and work together on what should be the most important project in their lives – raising their children to be responsible adults.

The traditional family was once the bedrock of American society, providing a strong sense of security for children, as they learned about life. Sadly, the traditional family in America has suffered under the relentless assault of the entertainment industry, which has, in recent years, created an onslaught of movies and television shows that ridicule such families as being a thing of the past. In Israel, however, the traditional family is still the foundation, and it's been getting stronger in recent years, despite the often negative influence of the internet and the obsession with smart phones, which as any parent will tell you, can get in the way of real communication.

Moral teaching and a firm family structure are both essential elements towards that goal, otherwise we are leaving our children in the unconstrained hands of internet and social media and they will naturally seek their guidance from wherever they can get it. Better for it to come from the home.

- Secure The Public Spaces

"Whoever saves a life of Israel, it is considered as if he saved an entire world."

(Mishnah Sanhedrin 4:5; Jerusalem Talmud 4:9, Babylonian Talmud Sanhedrin 37a)

Yes, it's speaking about Israel, but the principle is clear.

In Israel, where the threat to our children is mainly from Muslim terrorists, rather than from random crime and sick individuals, we have common sense solutions to the problem of shooting attacks in schools and other public places, and those principles can be applied in America. The basic principle here is to keep the guns in the hands of the good, stable, well-trained people, and only those who need it to protect themselves or others. For starters, not everyone can get a gun license and there are stringent background checks that can sometimes take weeks to investigate and process. Secondly, every school and most public buildings, and even some private ones, have a trained armed guard and sometimes several. In addition, there are sometimes school staff who are armed, and all are licensed after extensive background checks, with many being very well-trained in their capacity as members of local emergency response teams.

Furthermore, many schools and other public places also have security cameras. In fact, some communities in Judea and Samaria, which are adjacent to hostile Arab towns, have such cameras that encompass the entire perimeters of those communities to track terrorist infiltrations. Those extra security expenses are often covered by the local residents. Yes, it's an expensive one-time expense, but aren't our children worth the expense?

In the airports, it's time for some common-sense profiling. When a traveler arrives at check-in for flights on EL AL Israel Airlines, the security people already have done their background checks and know whether that person will need a more stringent examination. For example, an Arab who has recently traveled to Syria will be checked more stringently. Doesn't that make sense? Why should a 95-year-old grandmother, five generations in Montana, have to go through a random security check, while a 22-year-old Shiite Muslim from Pakistan waltzes past security?

Last, but not least, remember that violence and chaos usually occur when there is a vacuum of values. When there is no solid family/spiritual structure to provide those values, loneliness, chaos, anger and violence are given safe passage.

• Heal The Children

"You see a child play, and it is so close to seeing an artist paint, · *for in play a child says things without uttering a word. You can see how he solves his problems. You can also see what's wrong. Young children, especially, have enormous creativity, and whatever is in them rises to the surface in free play."* [7]

(Erik Erikson, American psychologist)

In recent years, Americans have suffered from more and more terror attacks. Whether these are organized attacks by terrorists inspired or directed by Islamic terror groups, or whether they are random attacks carried out by sick individuals, the results are similar. Post Trauma Stress Disorder, or PTSD, is very real and very widespread, and the victims who suffer the most are the children. Israel has vast experience in confronting terrorism, but not only through its capable security forces. The painful trauma of terrorism runs deep. After a terror attack, the discussion tends to be about the physical wounds, but the psychological wounds are much deeper, and often are noticed only much later, especially in children. The trauma reveals itself in a variety of symptoms, including fear of sleep, exaggerated aggression towards other children, and separation anxiety. Parents should explore the possibility of treatment for their children if these symptoms emerge.

The therapeutic programs supported by Shiloh Israel Children's Fund in the heartland of Israel use music therapy, art therapy, animal-assisted therapy, therapeutic horseback riding, movement therapy, biblio-therapy, and multi-sensory safe room therapy to heal the children. The vast experience gained from these treatments can and should be applied to American trauma victims as well.

• Recreate The Sabbath Day

"Remember the Sabbath day, to keep it holy. Six days you shall labor, and do all your work, but the seventh day is a Sabbath to the Lord your God."

(Exodus 20:8)

As described earlier, the Sabbath day (Shabbat or Shabbos) is a special day when observant Jews have a full day of rest, worship, and family engagement from Friday evening to Saturday night. The busy work week, and busy leisure and shopping weekend, is essentially set aside for an entire day. There are no computers, no televisions, and no cell phones; an island in time when all attention is focused on the family, along with the teachings of the Torah and its relevant commentaries that confront the important moral questions in our lives. It's a day when people actually eat together, sing together, and talk to each other in a relaxed, direct way, without sending text messages! Sunday was once a restful day in America when most stores were closed, and perhaps in some places it still is, but to a great extent, the Sabbath concept has been lost. Obviously, most Americans aren't Jewish and don't need to do it like we do, but wouldn't it be healthy to slow down a bit, and infuse some of these elements into the hectic, materialistic, and technologically heavy lifestyle?

• Speak With Your Accomplishments

"Say a little, do a lot."

(Ethics of the Fathers 1:15)

"Speak softly, and carry a big stick." [8]

(President Teddy Roosevelt)

It's no secret that President Trump likes to tweet and to say what's on his mind, but the truth is that he's been accomplishing a lot and many of his accomplishments have been done quietly. For example, hundreds of Obama era regulations that stranglehold businesses and choke the economy have been quietly removed and it hasn't been given that much media attention. This also applies to foreign policy. As President Trump has often said, he prefers not to speak about military actions being taken, nor those that will be taken in the future. The fact is that ISIS was decimated through very quiet, but decisive military action. With the very real challenges and threats from North Korea and Iran, it's hard to be quiet, but there, too, tit for tat threats aren't necessarily helpful. Yes, Trump will be Trump, and an effective politician does need to toot his horn once in a while, but the principle of modesty and quiet action is a good one, because when you speak less, the words that you do speak are more likely to be listened to.

• Welcome Good Immigration

"You shall also love the stranger, for you were strangers in the land of Egypt."

(Deuteronomy 10:19)

Yes, it's important to love and welcome the stranger, but not the hostile stranger. Not all immigrant groups have skills that can help America, not all immigrants want to be loyal Americans, and not all immigrants come from cultures with values that blend well with Western civilization. The Muslim mass immigration to Europe in recent years has brought countless problems, including a sharp rise in street crime and rapes of European women by Muslim men, an increase in terror attacks, and growing demands for the oppressive Islamic Sharia law.

We have seen signs of the same patterns in the United States, but to a smaller extent, because the percentage of Muslims in the US is still much smaller, although it's on the rise. President Trump's proposed immigration restrictions would help to reduce the danger. In short, no free country has an obligation to allow hostile immigration. As discussed earlier, immigration should be only for legal, hard-working, law-abiding and loyal potential Americans who will blend well in American society. And they should be welcomed in with open arms!

• Encourage American Creativity

"Israel is a perfect example of a country with which we should form closer bonds when we leave the EU: a growing and outwardly-focused, entrepreneurial nation with world-leading expertise in the industries of the future such as cyber, fintech, coding, and green finance." [9]

(Charles Bowman, Lord Mayor of London)

Jews succeeded in America by being creative and taking private initiative, such as establishing companies that started from scratch and rapidly grew to become great American success stories. Furthermore, the large number of Jewish Nobel prize winners has always been far disproportionate to the tiny Jewish percentage of the population.

That success has continued in the Land of Israel, as well. Since the early days that the Zionist pioneers drained the swamps to create agricultural settlements before the establishment of the State of Israel, Jewish creativity has been the engine that drives the country to its great accomplishments. In our times, Israel has become a high-tech leader far disproportionate to its size and numbers.

Nonetheless, the United States is still the homeland of free enterprise and private initiative and it used to lead the way in that sphere. That is what President Trump wants to and needs to unleash, in order to grow America once again. Having already slashed unnecessary regulations and excessive taxes that used to discourage private initiative, President Trump is off to a great start in restoring America's free enterprise system.

•   Destroy The Enemies Of Freedom

"The world is a dangerous place to live; not because of the people who are evil, but because of the people who don't do anything about it." [10]

(Albert Einstein)

"Victory at all costs, victory in spite of all terror, victory however long and hard the road may be; for without victory, there is no survival." [11]

(Winston Churchill, May 1940)

There are still countries in the world with regimes that clearly hate freedom and are doing everything in their power to spread their ideologies and develop nuclear weapons with malicious intent. Iran is one such nation, and its regime is developing long-range intercontinental ballistic missiles, with the evil intent of hitting the United States with nuclear weapons. If it comes to war, how should the United States respond?

While it's true that the world has changed in many ways, Israel's example of the Six Day War is a model for the world of how to fight a war – hit the enemy fast and hard, and on all fronts – economically, yes, but ultimately, militarily, and then fight to win. Yes, I know that most countries don't win a war in six days, but that is part of the miracle of modern day Israel. In our recent wars in Lebanon and Gaza, we have been less decisive and obsessively worried about hurting the enemy civilians. The Palestinian terrorist organizations exploited that to their advantage, placing rockets and other weapons in schools and hospitals, while daring Israel's reluctant leaders to attack. The results speak for themselves, as another war is unfortunately on the horizon.

The allies' strategy in World War II is another good example that both Israel and the United States should learn from. Hit 'em hard and understand that civilians will be killed in the fighting. It may not be the goal, but it can't be allowed to hamper the war strategy. No one likes war, especially those who have suffered significantly from war, as Israel has, but a war that is not fought 100% to win decisively is destined to be lost.

It would be nice to think that sanctions will do the trick, but in a global economy in which not everyone is on the same page, it can only weaken the enemy, but in most cases, it will not defeat him. Ultimately, evil must be confronted and defeated in the fullest sense.

- Stand with Israel

"And I will bless those that bless you, and him that curses you I will curse: and all the nations of the earth will be blessed through you."

(Genesis 12:3)

Nations that have supported Israel and/or have welcomed Jews in their countries through history have thrived. Look at Poland in the Middle Ages with its thriving commerce powered by Jews who were heavily involved in commerce. Look at Spain in the late Middle Ages, often known as the Golden Age of Spain, when Jewish life flourished in that country. Once they turned on their Jews, it was never the same. And look at the USA, which became the world leader, and has been good to the Jews and supportive of Israel. President Trump may not be an evangelical Christian on the emotional level of a Mike Pence or a Mike Huckabee, but he "gets it". He understands that the Israel-US alliance is good for Israel, but also for America, not just because of the valuable intelligence that Israel shares with America, and not just for the purpose of having a bastion of freedom and democracy in the Middle East. It's good to stand with Israel on a spiritual level, because it's good for America. Those who stand with Israel will be blessed, and doesn't America need God's blessings?

Keeping the Promise: On May 14, 2018, with many American and Israeli dignitaries present, a new plaque was unveiled dedicating the formal move of the US Embassy to Jerusalem.

- ## Make America Great Again

"Everyone has inside of him a piece of good news. The good news is that you don't know how great you can be! How much you can love! What you can accomplish! And what your potential is!" [12]

(Anne Frank, child Holocaust victim)

The Jewish people are not just a religion like other religions, nor is Israel a nation like other nations. We are a religio-nation, a chosen people with a unique mission to be a light unto the nations. While it is true that not every Jew will live in Israel, every Jew who wants to be connected to his roots must be connected to Israel.

"It's clear to me that one can't be Jewish without Israel. Religious or non-religious, Zionist or non-Zionist, Ashkenazi or Sephardic – all these will not exist without Israel." [13]

(Legendary Holocaust survivor and author Elie Wiesel)

From our lowly condition in almost two thousand years of exile, Israel has emerged – with an energy, a vibrancy, and an optimism that rivals any nation in the world. Even when we were suffering under slavery in Egypt or being slaughtered in the Nazi death camps, we always had an incredible optimism that things were going to improve. The quote above from the teenage Holocaust victim Anne Frank reflects that resilience that the Jews have always possessed, despite everything.

That optimism that Israel possesses in abundance is what Donald Trump is bringing back to America. Israel's lesson for America is that the level of greatness that one can achieve is not dependent on the depths to which one has fallen. All that's needed is a clear vision, the willingness to work hard, the humility to learn from others and to work to improve ourselves, and yes, the faith in the God of Abraham, Isaac, and Jacob that He will help us to achieve our lofty goals.

Working together, Israel and America, nothing is beyond our grasp!

Endnotes

(The author's online sources and references listed in the Endnotes include the complete linkage. The links were all connectable at the time of the publication of the first edition.)

Chapter One – Founders, Presidents, And The Jews

1. http://www.jewishvirtuallibrary.org/u-s-presidential-quotes-about-jewish-homeland-and-israel-jewish-virtual-library#lincoln

2. http://www.independent.co.uk/news/world/middle-east/barack-obama-israel-palestine-comments-occupation-settlements-cannot-be-permanent-a7319956.html

3. http://jewishnews.timesofisrael.com/trump-quotes/

4. http://www.jewishpathways.com/jewish-history/jews-and-founding-america

5. https://www.breakingisraelnews.com/98265/thanksgivings-dark-origins-puritans-believed-replacing-jewish-covenant/#VFzW5CxVmpe8Fycl.99

6. http://www.jewishpathways.com/jewish-history/jews-and-founding-america

7. https://www.breakingisraelnews.com/98265/thanksgivings-dark-origins-puritans-believed-replacing-jewish-covenant/#VFzW5CxVmpe8Fycl.99

8. http://www.jewishpathways.com/jewish-history/jews-and-founding-america

9. Ibid.

10. http://www.beliefnet.com/resourcelib/docs/115/message_from_john_adams_to_the_officers_of_the_first_brigade_1.html

11. https://www.monticello.org/site/jefferson/quotations-jefferson-memorial

12. http://www.beitbresheet.com/Heritage/Heritage.htm 21

13. http://www.resistnet.com/profiles/blogs/rebellion-to-tyrants

14. Rubin, David. *The Islamic Tsunami: Israel and America in the Age of Obama.* Jerusalem, Israel, 2010: 28-31.

15. http://www.leaderu.com/orgs/cdf/onug/franklin.html

16. http://www.jewishvirtuallibrary.org/u-s-presidential-quotes-about-jewish-homeland-and-israel-jewish-virtual-library#lincoln

17. http://en.wikipedia.org/wiki/Haym_Solomon

18. http://www.mickveisrael.org/museum-and-tours/the-story-of-mickve-israel

19. http://www.azquotes.com/quote/1310744

20. http://www.azquotes.com/author/91-John_Quincy_Adams

21. Denis, Brian. *The Elected and the Chosen*. Gefen Publishing House, Jerusalem, Israel, 2012: 100.

22. Benson, Michael T. *Harry S. Truman and the Founding of Israel*. Praeger Publishers, 1997: 191.

23. Ibid., 190.

24. Ibid., 191.

25. http://en.wikipedia.org/wiki/Iranian_Revolution, http://en.wikipedia.org/wiki/Iranian_Revolution
https://en.wikipedia.org/wiki/Trump_Village

Chapter Two - *The Obama Years*

1. https://www.washingtontimes.com/news/2015/jun/2/obama-i-am-closest-thing-jew-has-ever-sat-oval-off/

2. https://www.brainyquote.com/quotes/martin_luther_king_jr_115056

3. Obama, Barack. *Dreams from My Father: A Story of Race and Inheritance.* Three Rivers Press, 1995, 2004.

4. http://www.azquotes.com/quote/544201

5. https://obamawhitehouse.archives.gov/the-press-office/2012/09/25/remarks-president-un-general-assembly

6. Weiner, Justus Reid. "My Beautiful Old House and Other Fabrications by Edward Said." Commentary Magazine, Sept. 1999.

7. https://en.wikipedia.org/wiki/Bill_Ayers

8. http://www.nytimes.com/2001/09/11/books/no-regrets-for-love-explosives-memoir-sorts-war-protester-talks-life-with.html

9. www.wnd.com , Feb. 24, 2008.

10. Wallstein, Peter. "Allies of Palestinians see a friend in Obama." Los Angeles Times, Apr. 10, 2008.

11. http://abcnews.go.com/Blotter/DemocraticDebate/story?id=4443788

12. Ibid.

13. https://en.wikipedia.org/wiki/Jeremiah_Wright_controversy

14. http://www.jewishvirtuallibrary.org/jewish-voting-record-in-u-s-presidential-elections

15. https://www.space.com/8725-nasa-chief-bolden-muslim-remark-al-jazeera-stir.html

16. http://www.telegraph.co.uk/news/worldnews/barackobama/7521220/Obama-snubbed-Netanyahu-for-dinner-with-Michelle-and-the-girls-Israelis-claim.html

17. http://news.bbc.co.uk/2/hi/middle_east/7783325.stm

18. https://www.reuters.com/article/us-palestinians-israel/clinton-berates-netanyahu-over-settlements-idUSLDE62B28W20100312

19. http://www.newworldencyclopedia.org/entry/Temple_of_Jerusalem

20. https://www.nytimes.com/2016/12/28/us/politics/john-kerry-israel-palestine-peace.html

21. https://www.reuters.com/article/us-palestinians-israel-bush/bush-israel-settlement-expansion-impediment-idUSWAT00861920080103

22. https://www.huffingtonpost.com/alan-elsner/on-settlements-israel-has_b_10833536.html

23. http://www.washingtonpost.com/wp-dyn/content/article/2009/05/23/AR2009052301536.html

24. http://www.jpost.com/Arab-Israeli-Conflict/Leaked-document-claims-UN-anti-settlement-resolution-orchestrated-by-US-PA-co-op-476736

25. https://www.cnsnews.com/blog/michael-w-chapman/poll-63-israelis-rank-president-obama-worst-israel-last-30-years

Chapter Three – A Campaign Like No Other

1. https://www.brainyquote.com/quotes/john_
podhoretz_484825?src=t_political_campaign

2. https://www.timesofisrael.com/revealed-the-mystery-kibbutz-that-
once-hosted-bernie-sanders/

3. http://www.nationalreview.com/article/442739/keith-ellison-
islamic-radical-may-head-democratic-party

4. https://www.timesofisrael.com/election-2016-the-top-jewish-
moments-of-a-delirious-campaign/

5. https://forward.com/news/breaking-news/350837/donald-trump-
and-hillary-clinton-spar-over-iran-nuclear-deal-at-debate/

6. https://www.reuters.com/article/us-palestinians-israel/clinton-
berates-netanyahu-over-settlements-idUSLDE62B28W20100312

7. https://www.realclearpolitics.com/video/2015/03/23/liberty_
university_crowd_cheers_for_30_seconds_when_ted_cruz_says_
he_will_stand_with_israel.html

8. https://fivethirtyeight.com/features/how-the-republican-field-
dwindled-from-17-to-donald-trump/

9. http://www.nytimes.com/1999/06/26/nyregion/fred-c-trump-
postwar-master-builder-of-housing-for-middle-class-dies-at-93.html

10. Ibid.

11. https://www.washingtonpost.com/politics/2016/live-updates/
general-election/real-time-fact-checking-and-analysis-of-the-first-
presidential-debate/fact-check-how-much-help-did-trumps-father-
give-his-son/?utm_term=.41e5bf9d631a

12. http://www.nytimes.com/1999/06/26/nyregion/fred-c-trump-
postwar-master-builder-of-housing-for-middle-class-dies-at-93.html

13. http://www.politifact.com/truth-o-meter/article/2016/sep/09/
should-US-have-kept-Iraq-oil/

14. https://twitter.com/realdonaldtrump/status/679410900751802368
?lang=en

15. https://www.cbsnews.com/pictures/wild-donald-trump-quotes/14/

16. https://fivethirtyeight.com/features/how-the-gop-became-a-pro-
israel-party/

17. http://www.nytimes.com/1981/10/15/world/around-the-world-
khomeini-urges-export-of-iranian-revolution.html

18. https://www.rt.com/usa/336382-trump-aipac-rabbis-protest/

19. Ibid.

20. https://www.timesofisrael.com/trump-wins-over-aipac-with-true-
friend-of-israel-speech/

21. Ibid.

22. Ibid.

23. Ibid.

24. https://www.christianquotes.info/quotes-by-author/john-quincy-adams-quotes/#axzz54Z6Nhfs7

25. Ibid.

26. https://www.brainyquote.com/quotes/mike_pence_411934

27. https://www.brainyquote.com/quotes/mike_pence_412054

28. http://www.nationalreview.com/article/434142/donald-trump-good-father

29. https://www.washingtonpost.com/news/the-fix/wp/2017/11/27/trump-is-reportedly-saying-the-access-hollywood-tape-was-fake-news-he-should-talk-to-2016-trump/?utm_term=.6b623147ddb3

30. Ibid.

31. https://www.nytimes.com/2016/08/21/us/politics/hillary-clinton-presidential-campaign-charity.html

32. https://ballotpedia.org/2016_presidential_candidates_on_the_Iran_nuclear_deal

33. Ibid.

34. Ibid.

35. https://www.haaretz.com/.premium-polls-israelis-strongly-oppose-iran-deal-1.5386132

36. http://edition.cnn.com/2017/03/09/politics/west-bank-friedman-beit-el/index.html

37. https://www.haaretz.com/israel-news/.premium-what-does-trumps-negotiator-think-about-a-two-state-solution-1.5478326

38. https://www.nytimes.com/elections/results/president

39. http://www.businessinsider.com/world-leaders-reaction-donald-trump-election-2016-11/#israel-9

40. Ibid.

41. http://www.businessinsider.com/world-leaders-reaction-donald-trump-election-2016-11/#palestine-10

42. http://www.businessinsider.com/world-leaders-reaction-donald-trump-election-2016-11/#iran-11

Chapter Four – American Jews – Who Are They?

1. https://www.brainyquote.com/quotes/mike_gallagher_798826
2. http://www.davidrubinisrael.com/the-dennis-miller-show/
3. https://www.myjewishlearning.com/article/jewish-immigration-from-eastern-europe/
4. Ibid.
5. Ibid.
6. Rubin Family History.
7. https://www.myjewishlearning.com/article/jewish-immigration-to-america-three-waves/
8. http://bilerico.lgbtqnation.com/2012/06/american_conservative_judaism_approves_same-sex_we.php
9. https://www.timesofisrael.com/reform-movements-challenge-protesting-trump-and-remaining-inclusive/
10. Interview with Larry Feinstein – February 14, 2018.
11. https://www.brainyquote.com/quotes/gilbert_gottfried_555484
12. https://www.brainyquote.com/authors/matisyahu
13. The study was conducted by two leading scholars of American Jewry: Sylvia Barack Fishman of Brandeis University and Steven M. Cohen of Hebrew Union College. It analyzes data published in the landmark 2013 survey of American Jewry published by the Pew Research Institute.
14. https://www.haaretz.com/us-news/.premium-report-intermarriage-threatenes-u-s-jewry-s-future-1.5482043
15. https://www.israelnationalnews.com/News/News.aspx/221990
16. http://www.pewforum.org/2013/10/01/chapter-2-intermarriage-and-other-demographics/
17. https://www.israelnationalnews.com/Articles/Article.aspx/21715
18. http://www.pewforum.org/2015/08/26/a-portrait-of-american-orthodox- jews/
19. Ibid.
20. https://www.israelnationalnews.com/News/News.aspx/221990
21. http://religionnews.com/2017/09/13/most-us-jews-oppose-trump-but-the-orthodox-stick-with-him/
22. http://jewishweek.timesofisrael.com/orthodox-jews-emerging-as-trumps-truest-believers/
23. https://www.israelnationalnews.com/News/News.aspx/250068
24. http://jewishweek.timesofisrael.com/orthodox-jews-emerging-as-trumps-truest-believers/
25. http://www.pewforum.org/2015/08/26/a-portrait-of-american-orthodox-jews

Chapter Five – The New Jews And Trump

1. https://www.reddit.com/r/The_Donald/comments/59ghyx/i_only_work_with_the_best/

2. http://www.azquotes.com/quote/591457

3. https://www.timesofisrael.com/israel-employs-double-legal-standard-in-west-bank-us-envoy-charges/

4. Ibid.

5. http://www.nytimes.com/1984/10/27/nyregion/reagan-woos-jewish-voters-on-li-visit.html

6. https://patch.com/new-york/fivetowns/long-island-native-trumps-pick-ambassador-israel

7. http://www.ktvu.com/news/trump-pick-for-ambassador-to-israel-has-all-sides-on-edge

8. https://www.timesofisrael.com/after-friedman-nod-state-dept-reaffirms-support-for-two-states-calls-settlements-illegal/

9. https://www.timesofisrael.com/ivanka-trump-happy-to-be-jewish/

10. https://www.ynetnews.com/articles/0,7340,L-4099803,00.html

11. Ibid.

12. Ibid.

13. Ibid.

14. https://www.haaretz.com/us-news/jewish-journalist-takes-on-trump-s-immigration-advisers-with-genealogy-1.5752212

15. https://www.hollywoodreporter.com/news/how-trump-adviser-stephen-miller-divided-a-santa-monica-synagogue-989250

16. prnewswire/.../cair-franklin-graham-repeats-attack-onislam-79097332.html

17. San Ramon Valley Herald report of a speech to California Muslims in July 1998; quoted in Daniel Pipes' NY Post article, CAIR: Moderate Friends of Terror, Apr. 22, 2002.

18. Moore, Art. "DC Imam declares Muslim takeover plan." WorldNetDaily, May 10, 2010.

19. https://www.timesofisrael.com/stephen-miller-reportedly-writing-trumps-speech-on-islam/

20. Talmud, Ned. 28a, Git. 10b, BK 113a, BB 54b-55a.

21. A Compilation of the Messages and the Papers of the Presidents 1789-1897 Vol. IX, 198.

22. https://www.jta.org/2018/04/03/news-opinion/jewish-civil-rights-groups-file-brief-with-supreme-court-against-trump-travel-ban

23. https://www.israelnationalnews.com/News/News.aspx/244065

24. http://www.foxnews.com/politics/2018/06/26/supreme-court-upholds-trump-travel-ban-on-some-muslim-majority-nations.html

Chapter Six – Far Left and Far Right: Two Poles of Intolerance

1. https://www.brainyquote.com/quotes/hillary_ clinton_676724?src=t_extremism

2. http://www.latimes.com/nation/politics/trailguide/la-na-trailguide-updates-transcript-clinton-s-full-remarks-as-1473549076-htmlstory. html

3. Horowitz, David. *Barack Obama's Rules for Revolution: The Alinsky Model.* David Horowitz Freedom Center. Sherman Oaks, CA, 2009.

4. https://en.wikipedia.org/wiki/Occupy_movement

5. http://www.foxnews.com/us/2011/11/09/rash-sex-attacks-and-violent-crime-breaks-out-at-occupy-protests.html

6. https://www.voanews.com/a/muslim-groups-back-occupy-wall-street-protesters-132374778/147060.html

7. https://www.shabak.gov.il/SiteCollectionImages/english/ TerrorInfo/hlf09_report_en.pdf

8. https://www.forbes.com/sites/mattkibbe/2011/10/19/occupy-wall-street-is-certainly-no-tea-party/#240e7b19330c

9. https://www.commentarymagazine.com/articles/occupy-wall-street-and-the-jews/

10. Ibid.

11. https://www.reuters.com/article/us-usa-trump-inauguration-protests/violence-flares-in-washington-during-trump-inauguration-idUSKBN1540J7

12. https://www.nytimes.com/2017/08/01/opinion/womens-march-progressives-hate.html

13. https://twitter.com/lsarsour/status/598327052727615488?lang=en

14. https://www.nytimes.com/2017/08/01/opinion/womens-march-progressives-hate.html

15. Ibid.

16. Ibid.

17. Ibid.

18. Ibid.

19. https://www.israelnationalnews.com/News/News.aspx/245591

20. https://www.nytimes.com/2017/08/01/opinion/womens-march-progressives-hate.html .

21. Ibid.

22. http://insider.foxnews.com/2018/02/08/linda-sarsour-chuck-schumer-tired-white-men-negotiating-backs-people-color

23. http://www.foxnews.com/us/2017/08/12/emergency-declared-ahead-unite-right-rally-in-virginia.html
    https://en.wikipedia.org/wiki/Unite_the_Right_rally

24. http://edition.cnn.com/2017/08/14/politics/charlottesville-nazi-trump-statement-trnd/index.html

25. Ibid.

26. http://www.businessinsider.com/gary-cohn-upset-disgusted-trump-charlottesville-press-conference-2017-8

27. https://www.usatoday.com/story/news/politics/onpolitics/2017/08/25/trump-economic-adviser-gary-cohn-neo-nazis-wont-cause-jew-leave-his-job/601005001/

28. https://www.gatestoneinstitute.org/8956/black-lives-matter-antisemitism

    https://www.timesofisrael.com/black-lives-matter-platform-author-defends-israel-genocide-claim/

29. https://www.rushlimbaugh.com/daily/2017/08/14/what-really-happened-in-charlottesville/

30. https://books.google.co.il/books?id=RB8fCH_iaoQC&pg=PA79&l pg=PA79&dq=john+daly+skinheads&source=bl&ots=k8ZbcULE gN&sig=uWpW8YBKzjmAw7BH072YSwBBHFA&hl=iw&sa=X &ved=0ahUKEwiV6-3UmJbbAhVnMJoKHdbnAKM4ChDoAQh TMAY#v=onepage&q=john%20daly%20skinheads&f=false

    https://www.tamuhillel.org/jewish_ex-neo-nazi_promotes_education/

31. Interview with John Daly: February 13, 2018.

32. http://www.foxnews.com/politics/2018/01/03/dnc-deputy-chair-keith-ellison-signals-support-for-antifa.html

33. http://dailycaller.com/2016/11/17/democrats-must-scrutinize-keith-ellisons-anti-semitic-past-and-ties-to-radical-islam/

34. http://dailycaller.com/2018/02/09/three-democrats-rouhani-louis-farrakhan/

35. https://forward.com/news/national/404213/alexandria-ocasio-cortez-israel-democrat-future/

36. http://www.foxnews.com/politics/2018/06/25/trump-officials-hounded-and-harassed-as-protester-tactics-take-turn.html

37. https://www.dailywire.com/news/32228/watch-shouting-and-spitting-lefty-protesters-hound-ryan-saavedra

Chapter Seven – The Land Of Israel And Peace

1. https://www.brainyquote.com/quotes/benjamin_netanyahu_416717
2. https://www.brainyquote.com/quotes/winston_churchill_135259
3. Rubin, David. "Peace For Peace: Israel in the New Middle East". Shiloh Israel Press. Jerusalem, 2013.
4. http://en.wikiquote.org/wiki/David_Ben-Gurion
5. Rubin, David. "Peace For Peace: Israel in the New Middle East". Shiloh Israel Press. Jerusalem, 2013.
6. Twain, Mark. "The Innocents Abroad.", 1869.
7. Rubin, David. "Peace For Peace: Israel in the New Middle East". Shiloh Israel Press. Jerusalem, 2013.
8. http://www.zionism-israel.com/dic/Haj_Amin_El_Husseini.htm http://en.wikipedia.org/wiki/Haj_Amin_al-Husseini Schwanitz 2008 citing Abd al-Karim al-Umar (ed.), Memoirs of the Grand Mufti, Damascus, 1999, p.126
9. http://www.mfa.gov.il/mfa/aboutisrael/history/pages/israels%20 war%20of%20independence%20-%201947%20-%201949.aspx
10. www.mythsandfacts.com/conflict/10/resolution-242.pdf
11. Ibid.
12. Ibid.
13. Ibid.
14. Der Spiegel, November 5, 1969.

Chapter Eight – Palestinians, Peace And Reality

1. http://www.mfa.gov.il/MFA/ForeignPolicy/MFADocuments/Yearbook2/Pages/40%20Decisions%20of%20the%20Arab%20Summit%20Conference-%20Rabat-.aspx

2. https://www.brainyquote.com/quotes/yasser_arafat_178960

3. http://www.time.com/time/specials/2007/article/0,28804,1644149_1644147_1644129,00.html

4. http://www.iris.org.il/quotes/joburg.htm

5. http://jcpa.org/paying-salaries-terrorists-contradicts-palestinian-vows-peaceful-intentions/

http://www.jpost.com/Israel-News/Defense-Ministry-weak-on-fighting-Palestinian-pay-for-slay-MKs-say-542381

6. http://www.jewishvirtuallibrary.org/comprehensive-listing-of-terrorism-victims-in-israel#2018

7. https://www.timesofisrael.com/abbas-admits-he-rejected-2008-peace-offer-from-olmert/

8. https://www.jewishquotations.com/page/7/

9. http://jewishnews.timesofisrael.com/trump-quotes/

10. Ibid.

11. https://www.israelnationalnews.com/News/News.aspx/247715

12. http://jewishnews.timesofisrael.com/trump-quotes/

13. https://www.timesofisrael.com/us-to-move-embassy-to-jerusalem-on-may-14-day-of-independence-declaration/

14. http://jewishnews.timesofisrael.com/trump-quotes/

15. https://www.israelnationalnews.com/News/News.aspx/243358

16. Ibid.

17. https://twitter.com/SenTedCruz?ref_src=twsrc%5Etfw&ref_url=http%3A%2F%2F

18. https://www.nytimes.com/2018/03/19/us/politics/supreme-court-plo-trump-terrorism-case.html

https://www.reuters.com/article/us-israel-palestinians-decision/u-s-court-voids-655-million-verdict-against-plo-over-israel-attacks-idUSKCN1161UU

https://pjmedia.com/trending/sokolows-16-year-fight-justice-comes-12-days-short/

19. https://forward.com/fast-forward/372102/trump-national-security-advisor-mcmaster-western-wall-israel/

20. https://www.timesofisrael.com/bringing-in-bolton-white-house-stiffens-stances-against-palestinians-iran/

21. https://www.timesofisrael.com/trumps-state-department-no-longer-calls-west-bank-occupied-in-annual-report/

Chapter Nine – Big And Little Satans

1. http://thehill.com/homenews/administration/351323-trump-iran-nuclear-deal-an-embarrassment

2. http://www.cnn.com/2012/03/08/world/meast/israel-iran-relations/index.html

3. http://en.wikipedia.org/wiki/Iranian_Revolution

4. http://en.wikipedia.org/wiki/Iran_hostage_crisis

5. http://www.nationalreview.com/articles/227772/fall-shah/peter-w-rodman

6. https://www.timesofisrael.com/israel-raises-hezbollah-rocket-estimate-to-150000/

7. February 11, 1979 (according to Dilip Hiro in The Longest War p.32) p.108 from Excerpts from Speeches and Messages of Imam Khomeini on the Unity of the Muslims.

8. https://en.wikipedia.org/wiki/Iran_hostage_crisis

9. http://news.bbc.co.uk/2/hi/middle_east/4260420.stm

10. https://www.cfr.org/backgrounder/state-sponsors-iran

11. https://www.theatlantic.com/international/archive/2015/03/Iranian-View-of-Israel/387085/

12. https://en.wikiquote.org/wiki/Ali_Khamenei

13. https://en.wikipedia.org/wiki/Joint_Comprehensive_Plan_of_Action

14. https://www.heritage.org/global-politics/commentary/the-iran-deal-4-big-red-flags-the-middle-east-and-the-world

15. https://www.timesofisrael.com/boosted-by-nuke-deal-iran-ups-funding-to-hezbollah-hamas/

16. https://www.gatestoneinstitute.org/11330/iran-hamas-hezbollah

17. https://www.theatlantic.com/international/archive/2017/10/iran-deal-trump-next/542379/

18. http://www.bbc.com/news/world-us-canada-41605412

19. Ibid.

20. https://edition.cnn.com/2018/01/09/middleeast/iran-protests-3700-arrested-intl/index.html

21. https://www.brainyquote.com/quotes/albert_einstein_143096

22. http://www.foxnews.com/world/2018/04/03/saudi-arabias-crown-prince-slams-obamas-iran-nuclear-deal-backs-israels-right-to-exist.html

23. https://www.nytimes.com/2018/05/08/us/politics/trump-speech-iran-deal.html

24. https://www.israelnationalnews.com/News/News.aspx/244584
25. http://www.foxnews.com/world/2018/05/10/israel-strikes-nearly-all-iranian-infrastructure-in-syria-after-iran-rocket-attack-minister-says.html
26. https://www.jpost.com/Middle-East/UK-Germany-back-Israeli-right-to-defensive-strikes-against-Iran-in-Syria-556077
27. https://www.alaraby.co.uk/english/news/2018/5/10/bahrain-israel-right-to-defend-itself-following-syria-strikes
28. http://www.jpost.com/Israel-News/Top-pilot-Israel-capable-of-striking-Iran-if-orders-given-550097

Chapter Ten – Eleven Suggestions For Trump (From The Jews)

1. http://www.jpost.com/Diaspora/This-teen-had-a-gender-neutral-bnei-mitzvah-544052

2. https://www.israelnationalnews.com/News/News.aspx/242719

3. https://www.pressreader.com/israel/jerusalem-post/20171207/281586650930903

4. Interview with Nancy Matlin, February 27, 2018.

5. https://www.timesofisrael.com/god-fearing-and-generally-happy-poll-reveals-the-israeli-ethos/

6. https://www.whatchristianswanttoknow.com/christian-presidential-quotes-22-awesome-sayings/#ixzz584H4MR3V

7. https://www.brainyquote.com/quotes/erik_erikson_539562?src=t_child

8. https://en.wikipedia.org/wiki/Big_Stick_ideology

9. http://www.cityam.com/279180/london-and-israel-working-together-advance-industries

10. https://www.brainyquote.com/quotes/albert_einstein_143096

11. https://www.brainyquote.com/quotes/winston_churchill_138231

12. https://www.brainyquote.com/quotes/anne_frank_121214

13. https://www.brainyquote.com/quotes/elie_wiesel_599789

Image Credits

Other Books By David Rubin

More Sparks From Zion
ISBN: 978-0-9829067-8-1

Available online at www.DavidRubinIsrael.com/books/
~ Phone orders 1-800-431-1579 ~ Or at a bookstore near you!

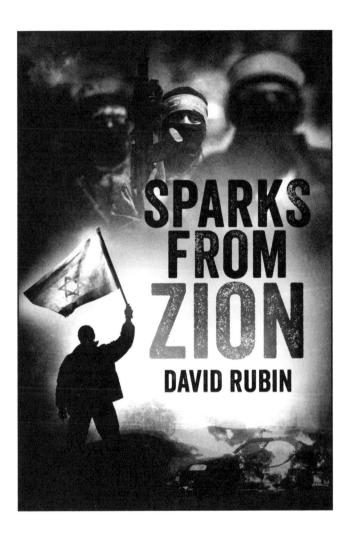

Sparks From Zion
ISBN: 978-0-9829067-6-7

Available online at www.DavidRubinIsrael.com/books/
~ Phone orders 1-800-431-1579 ~ Or at a bookstore near you!

Peace For Peace
Israel In The New Middle East
ISBN: 978-0-9829067-4-3

Available online at www.DavidRubinIsrael.com/books/
~ Phone orders 1-800-431-1579 ~ Or at a bookstore near you!

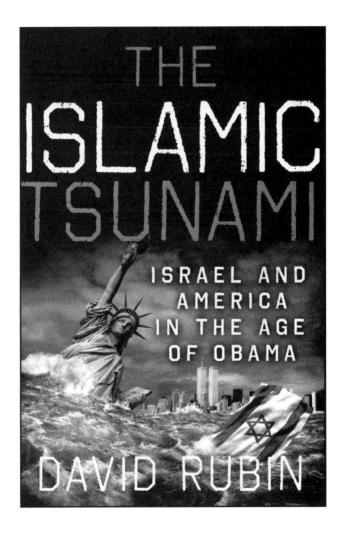

The Islamic Tsunami
Israel And America In The Age Of Obama
ISBN: 978-0-9829067-0-5

Available online at www.DavidRubinIsrael.com/books/
~ Phone orders 1-800-431-1579 ~ Or at a bookstore near you!

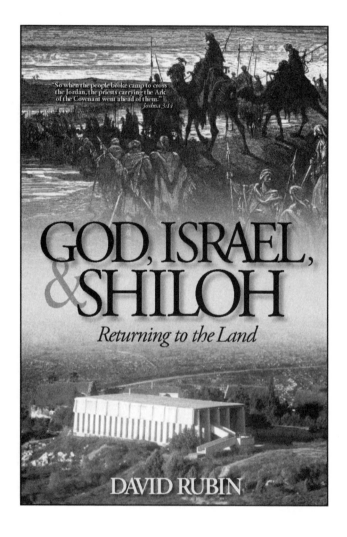

God, Israel, & Shiloh
Returning to the Land
ISBN: 978-0-9829067-2-9